POET ICONIC, VOL. 1

SELECTED POEMS
BY KELLEY ANN HORNYAK

Poet Iconic, Vol. 1
Copyright © 2019 by Kelley Ann Hornyak.

All rights reserved. No part of this book may be used or reproduced in any manner whatsoever without written permission except in the case of brief quotations embodied in critical articles or reviews.

For more information, contact:
www.poeticonic.com

Book and cover design by Kelley Ann Hornyak

ISBN: 978-1-7330326-0-5

First Edition: June 2019

10 9 8 7 6 5 4 3 2 1

For my many muses. Most especially those who are reading this.

TABLE OF CONTENTS

Introduction   1

2007

Rescue   5
Bookmark   7
Naked   9
Eight Thousand Days   10
Under Luna   11
Ruins   12
Queen of Strength, Sleep Silently   14
Carving Sunsets   16
Guilt of the Locust   17
Paper Gown   18
Early Departure   19
Love Is   20
Never So Far   21
Kiss You Hello   22
Breakfast with Aphrodite   23
Casualty   24

2008

The Same Waters   29
Palm Trees in the Wind   31
Dreamstrong   34
Nobody Abandoned Me   37
Shadows of the Creek   39
The Longest Wake   41
Bright Yellow Love   42

Drive	44
Pictures Painted	45
Nothing to Nature	47
Set the Stage	49
Fresh Eyes	51
If You Are Worth Loving	54
Paint	55
Love in the Present Tense	56
Where I Feel the Shame	58

2009

Frostbite	61
Good Enough on the Ground	63
Hope Personified	66
Closer to the Calm	68
Downpour	69
Loving the Broken Half of Me	70
Morning Came Without You	71
Haiku Interlude: Skin to Skin	73
Your Sky, Your Earth	74
The Killer of Dreams	75
Pioneer Glow	77
The Quiet	78
Ash and Dust	80
I Adore Us	82
Needed as We Are	83
The Mirror Image of the Wistful Star	85
Reliving	86
Skyscraper	87
The Messengers	88

2010

Torn Sky	93
While She Sleeps	94
To Stand Bare	95
You Wanted Me to Feel My Own Joy	96

2011

This Love is Greater	101
100 Proof	104

2014

Illegal Alien/Pearls Before Swine	109
Canyons	111
As Is	112
The Good Patient	113
Relief	114
Simple Solution	115
Until They Forgot	116
The Hopeful Place	117
Haiku Interlude: Tsunami Dreams	119
Who You'll Be Apart	120
The Speed of Life	122
Recollections/Destiny on Fire	124
November-Hearted	126
Haiku Interlude: Blood Moon	127
Bled	128
10,000 Nights	129
The Sea-Dweller and the Earth-Bound	130
The Baby, The Bathwater	131
Welcome	132
The Moment of Marriage	133
Haiku Interlude: Visionaries	136
Banshees	137
All Falls Together	139
Animals	141
Haiku Interlude: Nothing to Say	142
Travelogue	143
All the While Free	144
Diagnosis: Wrong	146
Restoration Complete	148
Haiku Interlude: Gardens of Dreams	149
8-Bit	150
Alchemists	153

2015

Growth	157
All That Matters	158

2016

Music in Me	161
A Few Words	163
Thin Air	164
Armor	166
A Lot Like Heaven	167
Oddlands	169
Eyes of Love	171
He Breaks the Night	172
Anxiety Creeps	173
Dream Maker	175
No Home	177
Know Peace	179
The Weight of Your World	181
Pacific	183
Walking Away Season	185
Her Religion is Love	187
Time Waves	190
Inborn	192
Spring	193
Soften Me	195
Passionflower	196
Love Note	198
I Have a Voice	199
Silent Movies	201
Walls Don't Talk (But We Should)	202
4 U	204
Every Blessed Thing	206
The Mourner and The Coroner	207
Cocoon	209
Take Life	210
Mask	211
Unauthorized	213
Turntables ('Round This Way)	215
Maimed	217

2017

Pearls	221
Weighted	223
Champion	224
Melancholy	226
The Square Circle	227
Disrupt the Night	228
Compliance	229
Good Enough Today	230
Amethyst	231
Sky-Bound	233
Old Haunts	234
Neon Beach	235
Brave	237
The Things I've Seen	238
Visible	240
Opposing Sides	241
Break	242
Bicoastal	243
Let Me Be	245
The Land of Loving Me	246
Peace & Ease	248
Hatchet	250
Discarding Darkness	252
Burn Bright	254
But I Breathe	256
Let It Shriek	258
Santa Barbara	260
Milk (Tread Carefully)	262
Hovel	264
The Laughing Girl and Me	267
Summer Trips	269
Skate or Die	270
Paper Dreams	271
Star Charts	272
Pass for Human	274
About the Author	277

INTRODUCTION

This collection is comprised of poetry posted on my blog, *PoetIconic.com*, and spans the decade from 2007 to 2017. This work centers on love and loss, healing and acceptance. I did not intend for this to be my first book, but seeing as I have poured my deepest trauma and most soaring joy into that online format for so very many years, it is long overdue that I bring this set of poems into the realm of physical print.

A bit of backstory. I've written melodies and lyrics ever since I could speak. I began writing poetry at age 13, when I was inspired by the poetry of Maya Angelou as read by Janet Jackson in the film *Poetic Justice*. Poetry was introduced to me through a pop culture lens. My teachers in this art of wordplay are the great pop/R&B songwriters and lyricists of the past few decades, including Michael Jackson, Mariah Carey, Prince, Beyoncé, and Ariana Grande. I have a voracious appetite for their words and I study them as if they were my gospel. If I am worthy of being their student, you will feel their influence pumping through these pages.

There is always so much I can express on paper that I cannot find the strength to speak out loud. The cover of this book is a visual representation of that feeling—of the sense of being silenced by an unwelcoming world. But open the book and let the words fly, and suddenly the poet's voice is free. The pages that follow will take you on a not-always-chronological journey through the loves and losses that make up a good life. As you know, poetry is as much about what the reader pulls from it as it is about what the writer puts into it. Sweet completion for me would be for these words to resonate with you, and to open up the same healing and acceptance in your world as it has in mine.

There are many more books within me. I hope you enjoy this first effort.

2007

RESCUE

I guzzle coffee, bitter and black.
Sugar could not sweeten me.
I like to keep it biting, bracing—
sour as the scowl on my lips.
My pain bleeds through cracks
in my sentences, spaces between
words that reveal far too much.
I have been naked and alone
even deep in commitment.
I keep miles between us
to keep me safe.
I am a bitch, a cruel overlord
who deprives her lover
of candles burning
and love unleashed.
I don't know how to be
sensuous and giving.
I have become the void,
the gaping emptiness
that sucks up all the light
and spits out nothing.
I escape.
I drive past her place,
note the flowers, remember
that she taught me to live.

Kelley Ann Hornyak

Still I wait in the cemetery
behind the black grave
that holds my pain,
beside the flat stone,
the understated marker
that says I loved my father.
I wait for the firetrucks to scream,
knowing I'm the only one
who can rescue me.

BOOKMARK

I curl up on the patio,
wrap one of my grandmother's quilts
around my shivering shoulders—
the ones that still bear
the world's weight.

I make a masterpiece with the stars,
connecting the dots in my mind.

I escape from it all for one evening—
melt into the sound of crickets singing,
let the fireflies dazzle my eyes.

The trees shimmer their leaves on down,
crinkling as they hand victory
to the cracked cement beneath.

We've all got to fall sometimes.

But I keep tripping
in the same old places,
and this is why I seek
the answers tonight.

I know that angels gather
around the flickering
wax sticks of flames.
I know they hear my prayers
and words of pain.

But nothing around here has changed,
so why do I keep coming back here
again and again?

"Why does the sun rise every day?
Some things just never change."

And if that is their answer,
then what can I say?

All I can do is sit on my
imaginary porch swing,
dreaming of possibilities
that only exist in my head.

I will cherish these
broken wings anyway,
as a souvenir
of what used to be—

as a bookmark
that keeps me
here on this page.

NAKED

Sexy
like a naked sentence.
Like our feelings
without the disgusting
pretense.
Like a creature
of nature
unbound by
civilization.
Rules and lies
made up to keep us
quiet... safe... scared.
My drugged brain
still stands and salutes
when you walk
into the room,
because instinctively
I know that you are truth.
This is sensuality,
the brutality of a life
without dishonesty.
I could never be
as open
as you.
But inspired?
Absolutely.
You wake me up
and set me ablaze.

Kelley Ann Hornyak

EIGHT THOUSAND DAYS

There is a pervasive sadness
in the constant seeking.

Like a lonely red ball,
rolling and bumping its way
down rainy cobblestone streets,
splashing in and out of cold puddles,
searching for the child who once
bounced it on sunny pavement.

I wanted the past
to return and comfort me,
to be reborn as a perfect future,
to answer the questions
and validate me.

Neither past nor future
moved to paint the theme.
The present kept its ancient hold,
and I learned to love its embrace.
I found constancy in the way
she always changes.

Today is beautiful.
I wish I had realized it
eight thousand days ago.

UNDER LUNA

Walking between the sound of rainfall and soft laughter, I slip through my sleepy solitude and find a clearing to rest in.

There are soft grasses and warm rocks to press my chilled skin against.

The stored sunlight toasts my cold core, though it is dark beneath the moon now, and a smile gently finds my lips. I am replenished, and ready to continue my life's trek.

RUINS

Lying there
in the cold shadow
of my own sanity,
I remembered
what it was like
to rest in the safety
of your ruins.

I was
no longer
privileged
to sleep
beneath
your
broken
wings.

I reached for the
alarm clock,
fumbled for the
snooze button,
worn off from
years of repeated
morning bashings.

I never wanted
to wake up.
But sober
and sanguine,
there I was.

Open sky
threatening.
My bare skin
felt raw
and wrong.
But God would
not wait for me
to feel better,
to feel good.

Life had to
go on.
Whether
here or gone,
whether
screams
or songs.

No late slips,
no excuses.
No loopholes,
no escapes.
I had to face
the mirror and
my singular
reflection.

Alone I faced it.
Alone I stand.

There is no greater pain
than learning
to walk this world
without you in it.

Kelley Ann Hornyak

QUEEN OF STRENGTH, SLEEP SILENTLY

In loving memory of Adeline Zambrowski (1919–2004)

Queen of strength, sleep silently.
I will keep watch.

Tonight I will take your place
and rule over all my eyes survey.
The knotted joints, twisted and tangled—
the wrinkled skin, so papery thin.
I'll wish it smooth and thick with life,
back in time as we're pitched through
days that dream of stealing you.

Queen of strength, sleep silently.
I will keep watch.

Tonight I'll toil to stop and stay
the tide that takes the soul away.
The labored breaths, so slow and strained—
the heart still beating, almost weeping.
I'll wish it fierce but full of peace,
rushing red through perfect veins,
youth removing stains of age.

Queen of strength, sleep silently.
I will keep watch.

I'll question our mortality
and dare command death far from thee.
We'll face the winds, though whipped and thrown,
clinging to the stars we've known.
I'll wish them to forever shine,
resisting time's unbending plan.
If you hear me, just squeeze my hand.

Queen of strength, sleep silently.
I'm still keeping watch.

CARVING SUNSETS

breaths slip out of raspberry-stained lips
on a screened-in country porch

some wasted forever, some fate-kissed

as the photographs singe and fade
like the words we etch in sunsets

in the life that follows this
we'll reclaim those blessed sentences
and they will light the sky

unending amber glow

the pain that breaks us here
will glorify

with each breath
i sink fast
into death

still i breathe

GUILT OF THE LOCUST

Decades wasted
with no justification.
I'm filled with concentrated
guilt, weighing more than
the years themselves.

After all, I was more than just lazy.
I hurled spite and hurtful slurs
at the ones who stayed with me
or attempted to save me from myself.

Time didn't tell me. It showed me.
The ones who then stayed
are the ones who remain,
though I often desert myself.

A wise friend shares a verse,
promising me that God will replace
all the years the locusts ate.
But what is heaven's verdict
when I consumed them myself?
I must shoulder the blame,
do the work it will take,
and swallow the extra pain.

My life still lies before me.
I dig in with sharpened claws,
at last understanding that
the only way to dull my ache
is to take the actions I avoid.

PAPER GOWN

Dedicated with love to Lisa Mendez

You never know how close you are to the gates
until you feel the breath slip from you.
Like letting go of that pretty balloon,
it's up, past the clouds, and gone far too soon.

I felt that thread lengthen and thin today
as you gasped for air and screamed for life.

I can't lose you now—not now that I've
finally realized that you are my heartbeat.

The center of my life
rests uncomfortably
behind sterile doors,
wrapped in a paper gown
and teetering dangerously close
to a place that I can't fathom.

Did you look in her eyes
when she fell in love with me?
Did you feel that heart pumping
when she fought for me?

I will it to continue beating.
Keep the rhythm strong
and the music sweet.

Let the one I love continue to breathe.
God, I need her here with me.

EARLY DEPARTURE

In loving memory of Roger Allen Hornyak, 1943–2003

Heavy greyness coats this day,
halfway between brightness and shadows.
It falls on the city like your moods once did.
They are moods I miss as I plot my life,
taking step after step without you.
Your absence has given my life more meaning—
a reason to look above and believe
that there is a place where you still live and breathe,
albeit in a different kind of way, I'm sure.
But I can't help the feeling
that your presence would have blessed me
just a bit more than your early departure.
Isn't it funny how you can watch something happening
and not understand it until later?
Despite that silhouette of questions unanswered,
I am blanketed in soft clouds of comfort,
knowing that you left a heartbreaking life behind,
moving on to a place where you understand the reasons why.
You deserve that peace and to hear what's true:
That I love you more than you ever knew.

Kelley Ann Hornyak

LOVE IS

Originally published in Family Equality Council's HEARTsongs, a collection of poetry written by LGBTQ families

Love is finding one who adores all we've become.
It is joining with that soulmate and
traversing sunny seas, then weathering the storms
to find the hard-earned joy within them.
Love is becoming a family, opening our homes.
It grows when we embrace and guide each other
to become more than what we were before —
to become better, warmer, and less alone.

NEVER SO FAR

More than a decade later and the tears still flow
when I remember the joy you brought me.
In a time of shadows
when I was confused and searching,
you were a diffused morning glow.
Like the sun's rays filtered
through frosted glass, your light was
bright enough to open my eyes
but not so bright that it would burn me.

You were one of the few who weren't poison
to this girl so fragile, to this sensitive life.
I am still on eggshells,
but now when I hear the soft crunch
I understand that I am only human.
Like the child you loved then,
I am slowly growing up.
Tall enough to reach the clouds
but not so tall that I forget what's beneath.

In both places, above and below, I find you.
You are spirit and ashes—wind and bone.
Reminding me quietly
to retrace the tracks we both left in the snow
and to take back the life that was once our own.
Like you did that morning,
I have to go back home.
Far enough to find the things I left there,
but never so far that you can't come with me.

KISS YOU HELLO

I want to see you radiant,
sun splashed in your hair,
skin dewy as morning.

I want to hear you sing,
notes of heaven in the air.

I want to touch your hand,
and feel your hand touch mine.

I want to know your love,
and show that open
does not mean broken.

I want to cherish your spirit,
your female warrior
and your little girl
alike.

I longed to know this state,
to touch it and keep it
and know it intimately.

And now I taste love
every day when I wake
and kiss you hello.

BREAKFAST WITH APHRODITE

This is euphoria,
a place I belong.
Aphrodite and I
eating breakfast
in our warm bed.
An escape artist
other than me
dangles defiantly
between this world
and the next.
We laugh.
The joke's on us,
but it's beautiful.
A letter arrives,
"You got the job."
Bills get paid and
I'm speechless
with gratitude.
Another month
with a roof over
our silly heads.
The newspaper
tells me where
I'll find success,
both astrological and
business sectional.
The forecast says
it'll be a clear day, but
storms are waiting.
We'll be ready.

CASUALTY

Quietly
reclaiming
everything
you stole
from me

in my own way,
without returning
to your space.

Discovering
a reality
that is better,
stronger,
and healthier

than any day
I ever coveted
from you.

This is,
after all,
a gift of
change.

And what
was gifted
will remain.

Hunger for
better things
pushes me
to try
harder

in my own time
without reverting
to old ways.

Empowering
possibilities
that soothe me,
heal me,
and teach me

more than they could
in ancient damaging
moments.

It was,
in the end,
a war I
won.

Every
casualty
now reborn.

2008

THE SAME WATERS

I can see your sparks ignite, flare, and fade.
Golden like September leaves, promise rings,
and the unfiltered sun that once burned me.

It now gently warms me, reminding me
   of words on paper now incinerated.
      I was never quite destroyed
although the pages
            went up in flames.

      It would take much more
      and still I would breathe,
   albeit quietly.

I was built for the blasts
   of nature's winds so angry.
      Though it's never quite easy,
      it's what's meant to be.

         So much older and a little wiser.
      Even so, I jump the clouds
   and skate on lightning bolts,
looking for that next high
   to get me through the fog
      of another day.

It's no sin to drink of
   those electric rivers,
      to sip the sounds
   of heaven that trickle down.

Kelley Ann Hornyak

I am moved.
   I too surge, flame, and die,
      leaving behind a pool of life
  for someone else to dive into.

A creative life's work that began with you...
   A connection forever etched in time...
      A very first touch that reaches me still...
though the jolt of youth is clearly gone.

   Forever changed, still the same.

   Always grateful to wade in
  the same waters
as you—

always better
  when you
    are here.

PALM TREES IN THE WIND

I still see our pink tropical sunrise,
majestic palm trees surging up
from the rich soil of our minds.
Pretty eyes, young and unafraid,
reminding me of days we left behind.
We're still, after all, two of a kind.

The glitter never washed away,
settling into sexy wrinkles
on ever-changing faces.
The shimmer sunk in,
and it stays there
just under our skin.
Nobody else can see it
but we know that it exists.
If we suds up
and scrub hard enough,
we might reveal it again.

And here we are bare, you and I,
twin goddesses of beautiful chaos.
Still searching, still yearning, never happy,
and blessed to be that way, because we know
intrinsically that satisfaction is stagnation.
We'll never reach sweet completion,
and that's our destiny, imperfect and free.

Kelley Ann Hornyak

Beneath the search there is a purpose,
a tangible reason that we were crafted
from dust and gifted with breath.
It was written in stone
that today we would have
hearts that still beat,
hands that still reach,
and lips that still sing,
though so quietly.

We've been taken apart
bit by bit, and it may be true
that we are unrecognizable now.
But there's a natural, mysterious pull
like the moon has over the tides,
eternal and unstoppable.
Soon enough we will find
ourselves whole and healed,
with faith and magic returned.
The two hearts with hairline fractures,
once believed to be shattered,
are now beginning to mend.

I step down off my tower,
for once bowing in respect
to the one who came before.
I am sorry that I was jealous and spiteful,
and I take responsibility for being
that insecure and willful child.
Crone, mother, and maiden, we stand.
Sometimes I think we are her daughters,
but you are somehow a nurturer to me.
I am still stumbling on my baby steps
while you falter with your growing dreams.
You pass the tiara and I hand it right back.
One day I will earn my own diamonds.
There's no glory if I steal them from you.

In this moment that we both own,
all I desire is for you to come home.
But please take your time and get here safely,
taking smaller steps and keeping your eyes fixated
on something higher than flashbulbs and paparazzi.
Keep your toes anchored to the earth beneath,
open your wings, and remember to stand tall.
Enveloped in prayers, angels kiss your face
and guide your steps back to where you belong.

I'm stronger for having known you,
and you are better for having taken the fall.

DREAMSTRONG

Been feeling so creative,
blessed with breath again.
Like my skin's on fire...
Jolt of electric you.
If I could bottle you up
and drink you each day,
this is what I'd be like...
but I guess I've got to
make my own breeze
to settle in under my wings
and help me fly.
Don't take too long,
keep your dreams strong,
live for the moment,
they're telling me.
I live their words
but they only hear
what others say,
but anyway,
I know better than to listen
to the tales they are spinning.
Dreams.
Take one down,
put your heart in the pocket,
keep it a while,
then pass it around.
If you hide that precious water
it can never cleanse their sins.
Pick yourself up
and walk outside sometimes.

The sun will tan the hurt away
and remind you of
your best days.
There's a place you can go
when you feel like
you've hit your low,
and the top notes
will lift you
back towards
the ceiling
where you
belong.
Break it.
The glass.
Let it shatter,
let it crash.
Everybody will recover,
but you will always regret it
if you don't find out
what's past it.
Might lose it all,
but then again
what are we really living for?
It's about taking chances
and making the changes.
You get what you earn,
and you don't grow
if you don't get burned.
Keep loving
even when you can't see
through your tears.
One day you'll evaporate
along with sadness
splashing down your cheeks,
and when you do,

you'll clasp your hands
and say, "Thank God
I did not settle
for any less."

NOBODY ABANDONED ME

Wishful when I
get close to that energy.
It enlivens me.

Tired of repeating words—
invoking the same phrases
to tell the same story
I've been telling
since time began.

Ego unconsciously clinging
to an identity of
pain and abandonment—
of "I am the victim."

But nobody abandoned me.

Life happened
and death interrupted.
It was an event—
something to learn from
and move past.

But stuck I stayed,
caught on loose ends,
clawing for the connections
that I thought comprised
the totality of me.

Kelley Ann Hornyak

Turns out—I am
an independent entity,
existing even without
a controversial history.

That is the definition
of irrelevancy.

When I wake tomorrow
I'll tell a present story,
dip into the current
and float there awhile.

Because not one moment
of yesterday defines me.
Circumstances unfold and fade.
No longer will they stay.

SHADOWS OF THE CREEK

A lapse in judgment,
a sacrifice in the name of what could be.
I try to tread on the rough, sturdy stones
but sometimes I slip on the slick, smooth ones.
The rain falls and the current crashes, splashes,
hitting me hard and knocking me back.
As I stand again, humbled again,
I remember again, I am only human.

A scratch here, a scar there,
like a checklist of faults
to return to and fix.
I promise myself tonight
to come back one day
and make it right.

I keep stepping across
the river stones,
stopping now and then
to brush the small, sharp rocks
out of the cuts on my knees.

Each imperfect try
marks a chapter of my life.

Kelley Ann Hornyak

Still I smile
in the shadows
of the creek—
with tears on my cheeks
and mud on my jeans—
because I am the creation
these mistakes make complete.

THE LONGEST WAKE

I used to believe in solidity and predictability.
I held fast to the concept that I held the reins—
that I could plan and execute a flawless destiny.
Don't get me wrong—there is something to be said
for hard work, faith, integrity, and belief.
But nothing can stop the pull of death,
the destruction it leaves, or the time it takes to grieve.
Denial steals years like cigarettes steal heartbeats.
Decades ripped from lives faster than you realize.
And all that loss... hauntingly lovely in the way
it wakes you from your slumbering stupor...
that endless loss returns cyclically to remind you
that you can take nothing for granted on this plane,
no matter how much love or money you accumulate.
So even if you work your fingers to the brittle bones beneath,
and run on empty, pushing your body past the call of sleep...
Remember this one thing as the hours fluidly creep:
The end that hovers—ominous and heavy—is the only guarantee.

BRIGHT YELLOW LOVE

Inspired by Shelley Krause

In this broken slice of a
tranquil blue-green morning,
bright yellow enthusiasm
leaps off your words
like fire off the sun.

It explodes,
falls back into itself,
and erupts with passion
again and again.

This is your love.

You raise him
with selfless smiles
of devotion.

Pure in heart,
no hidden motive.
Nothing to gain,
but everything
to give.

And as I watch you,
you live and breathe
so naturally
in the space
of parenthood.

I know that
it will be a while
before I can do
the same.

I don't have it to give,
because I haven't invested
in my own soul yet.

My own passion
has been flung wildly
from affection
to affection,
obsession
to obsession.

If I want to
one day
lose myself
in the life of
my child,
I have to
find myself
first.

I will observe
and one day
emulate—
but today
I explore
and wait.

DRIVE

Originally published in literary journal Andwerve

Coffee crept up my spine, so sleepy,
infusing my eyes with strength to pop open,
and if I was lucky, they'd stay that way.
I gave it fifty-fifty.
Half past, I climbed into my steel seclusion,
ripped the solitude I needed
from the lines slashed across the road.
Antenna imperceptibly bobbed
to the beat of saccharine—
sugar sweet melody clouded my frowning eyes,
guided the wheels to a place I should not have gone.
I reached for a tissue—found you.

PICTURES PAINTED

You are a delicious sight for these pained eyes,
just like clear water in a stretch of hot sand.
Difficult to believe so many years have gone.
I only mildly strayed, but so much changed.
Each return, a liminal ritual,
refreshing and healing me.

Your rain is warm, cleansing. Joyous.
Alone in you, I take you in,
and you make me more
than I can be on my own.

The crisp crackles of your lightning
still shock my senses and gently wake me
from depression-induced slumber.

Green sky hails a downpour,
and I watch from the shelter
of my raindrop-encrusted window,
aflutter like a young child of divorce
waiting for her daddy to pick her up
and go for ice cream.

The clouds open up like a storybook,
wet pages spilling heaven's ocean,
audible, crashing, splashing on the street.
Sunlight casts a glow of rich amber
through each droplet, cascading endlessly.

Kelley Ann Hornyak

I lay back on a bedspread of so many years
quilted from my love, your laughter, our prayers.
The sun shines through the window glass
and projects the wet cloud tears,
golden, on my skin and across the bed.

Pictures painted in vivid shades of sienna
and yellowed love letters from a faded past.
There is so much to touch, to kiss, to taste—
to remember and cherish all at the same time,
from our sugar-dusted yesterday
to the warm amaretto
of this afternoon
and early evening.

Wait for the rain to slow,
take it down to a whisper
and let me sink in.

NOTHING TO NATURE

Can you see the tides coming in as clearly as I can?
We've both been swimming out a long time,
but now we have to float a moment,
taper our efforts,
and enjoy a deserved rest in the midday sun.
Then we'll quickly dart with the current,
letting it nudge us deftly back to shore,
embracing whatever we find when we get there.

I have resisted everything for so long.
I've resisted change, resisted remaining the same.
I've fought hard against fate, to no avail.
These waters will not bend to my command,
and your reluctance means nothing to nature.
Your anchor is weightless to her.

She will crush your wishes and make her plans known,
not maliciously—just inevitably.
She speaks only what you least long to hear,
bluntly giving you precisely what you need
to change, to grow, to continue one more day.
She is fate, bubbling through the crests,
building to ice-cold sea splashes
that cleanse the beaches and your mind
of needless debris.

Kelley Ann Hornyak

It seems counterintuitive to swim back now. I know.
But when we set out on this watery trek,
we promised to stay true to the vision we held.
We swore on all that mattered to our naked souls
that we would never stray from that cherished image.
If reaching it means learning the backstroke
and a new way of being, then let's try.

We cannot know better than the creative forces
that shape us and pull us through time.
We can't second guess the winds or the storm fronts
that sweep through like divine brooms,
weeding out the dying parts
and breathing life
into the tiny new pieces.

The ecstasy is in the acceptance of change.
The yielding to it—the bending through it.
Our strength is found in our flexibility,
and wisdom is blended between age and youth.
Let's mermaid our way back through those waves
and find what we overlooked when we began.

SET THE STAGE

She begins
to set the stage—
to lay out the things
she thinks I'll need
to complete this act
after she exits,
leaving the spotlight
for me.

Uncomfortable
with that stillness,
with her lack of
resistance to time.
I whisper, "I know,"
but even now,
I really don't.

Countless hours spent
preparing myself,
imagining the blunt edges
of that morning or evening
that is, I pray, so far in the future
that I shouldn't be thinking of it yet.

Kelley Ann Hornyak

At 26, I could shave off the two.
I am still learning the basics.
Still alternating between
crawling and walking—
between soaring and falling.
I still need this hand to hold.
How can she be leaving?

Certain moments are aglow,
and I see then that I can survive,
even alone.

But there are still dark patches
and painful pieces I can't fix.
That contrast builds the scene,
and its stark blacks and whites
are surprisingly and unbelievably
lovely.

She taps my shoulder,
reminds me of something
that she has just learned herself—

no one wants to
hear the highlights
without the crashing lows.

I'm grateful
and growing
as she takes a bow.

FRESH EYES

Seemingly
unfair
somehow
that you
didn't get
a chance
to open
your
eyes.

I spoke
the words
but they
did not
stick,
and now
we'll never
know.

Kelley Ann Hornyak

Truth—
I should
not write
about you.
You were
so angry
and your
words
hurt so
many.
The
phrases
in death
will still
sting.

But I
remember
the better
days.
A time
when you
weren't
full of hate.

And I hope
that you
stand there
with her now,
seeing us all
with fresh eyes.
I hope there is
forgiveness
after this life.

And I hope
you found
a piece of that
when you arrived.

Kelley Ann Hornyak

IF YOU ARE WORTH LOVING

If you are worth loving,
you will not disappear when I need you the most.
That's been the theme. That's now my criteria.

When it rains, you seem taller, more protective.
You'll become my umbrella if there's no ceiling overhead.

I don't get lost in the fear that you might break me
when I'm at my most fragile, because even though you can,
I know with certainty you never would.

I am an integral, irreplaceable part of your world,
but I'll never be the whole of it.
There are other people, other places, other passions
that fill your days and nights with faith and light.

When I am lost in myself, you talk me through it,
but you don't force me to seek the light that blinds me.
You take it slow and coax me out with understanding.

Most of all, when I choose to shine,
you don't block the spotlight
or shut your eyes.
You just smile in the glow
and fill with pride.

If you are worth loving,
this is why.

PAINT

I am hanging up photos in my mind,
holding them high and paying respect
for all the tiny details that came together
to create these snapshots of a life.
They are pictures of the past and present
that now more than ever
explain who I am.
They do not define me anymore.
I define them.
But I see you glaring,
teeth gritted, fists clenched,
because you want me to be
what you want me to be—
nothing more and nothing less.
You fashion yourself the artist
and I suppose I'm the canvas,
but what you fail to notice
is the fact that there is
already a vivid portrait,
what may one day be a masterpiece,
painted intricately upon me.
You want to paint over it,
make it better,
make it perfect.
But I can tell you with certainty
that another coat of paint
will suffocate me.

Kelley Ann Hornyak

LOVE IN THE PRESENT TENSE

I dozed. I woke from an uncomfortable slumber
to realize I can't remember the last time I felt loved.

The joy that I feel for our union
is the joy that I feel over my own feelings for you.
It's never been joy over the things you do to lift me up,
or to help me heal, or to make me whole.

Those are tasks I have to take on myself
though I still dream of being rescued.
I know if I am, it won't be by you.

I understand all too well
that love in the present tense
has nothing to do with romance.

It seems, in my experience,
that it's about tolerance
and obedience.

And it's not just here at home—
I see that in all the couples I've known.

You stuff down your feelings,
you placate your partner,
you tell the lies
to get through the day.

I say I'm okay when I'm clearly not.
I say I'm over it when I'm still grieving.
I say I love only you
when over time I'm learning
that I have to love me too.

We will lash out, and we will
either transform or wither.
We will bend and grow,
or break and disintegrate.

If you leave,
you say I'll move on and love another.
I say I'll stay single for a good long while.
My reasons are deeper than you know.
You were the only one who was worth this pain—
worth this heavy chunk of life that's now gone.

I am old now, damaged and cynical—
and I'd break love if it hadn't broken me first.

Kelley Ann Hornyak

WHERE I FEEL THE SHAME

So this is where I feel the shame. The stunted wins of halfhearted games—the sour sting of heavy-handed blame. I deserve the hard lashes. I accept the sharp pain.

Yours is the heart that I covet. Glowing respect for promises I kept, not regret for what I haven't done yet. I still long for you, bashful. I receive rejection.

I learned so much then turned away. The graceful way that you saunter then sway—emulating your style to fade away. I called for something lasting. I accept three short days.

Now all we have is this moment. Not enough to make world-shifting attempts, but maybe enough to make one dent. At last, I am accountable. Ready to choose once again.

2009

FROSTBITE

Tiny ice crystals coat each narrow branch
that grows tentatively from the tree
where our initials were never carved.
It's a soft freeze—
barely perceptible
to the naked eye,
but that thin layer of frozen dew
has been enough to hinder movement
for seventeen long years.

If you walk a little further,
down to the ocean's edge,
you'll find the places
where entire waves
have frozen mid-splash.

A few steps up the beach—
the house—with the room
where we skirted destiny.
I can no longer enter—
if I did, I'd have to creep in
just as silently as we did then,
and today, I'd be alone.
These spaces,
no matter how well loved,
no longer belong to us.

Kelley Ann Hornyak

Through the bright white noise
there are dark and lonely cries,
each time a bit more desperate
than the time before.
These too are subject to the frost—
haunting digital frozen waves.

Wouldn't some
coffee and cigarettes
melt it all away?
All the snow,
all the distance,
all the years of waste.
If your smoke curled
around my latte mug
while you laughed
at the things I'd say.

But no matter how much I lament these
scratches in my iced-over rear-view mirror,
I understand somewhere deep down
that I am better for the damage.
More real—more human.
Much more loving—so much changed.

And still, the water flows toward you.
Even uphill it will make its seasonal trek.
One day it will be warmed by sunlight
instead of solidified by the cold.
Tonight I settle into the shiver,
the frostbite taking me over.

GOOD ENOUGH ON THE GROUND

I was born with my eyes on the sky,
wings aching to beat against the wind
and carry me to join
the other songbirds way up high.

My cravings were pure and authentic then.
I was connected to the life that flows through everything,
and I knew my place—understood my worth.

The song came first
and is more intrinsic to me
than anything else
I may cling to today.

Long before the world tried to break these wings,
I was already looking for reasons and excuses not to fly.
I was afraid of failure, afraid of success—
unsure that I was strong enough to withstand either possibility.

Kelley Ann Hornyak

You came along and awakened new parts of me.
Love softened all the blows of the past,
and I longed for the normalcy that came so naturally to you.
When you shared your standards—a home, a family, no flights of fancy—
the left hemisphere of my brain shouted yes.
Yes to the security, yes to the classic American dream.
I was painting the picket fence white before we even bought these rings,
tucking my wings painfully inside a wedding dress
before either of us got down on one knee.
I wanted to embody what you desired of me.
I failed miserably.

Over and over again—three times at least, stretched over 12 years—
I tried to rip out my dreams as they kept growing like weeds.
More times than that, I tried to leave,
but found that these aspirations were empty
without your arms surrounding me.

My fingernails scraped the hard earth and I began to lose my grip.
Face pressed into the side of the cliff, I tasted my own tears.
At the end of my strength, when I could hold on no longer,
I could either let go of the ledge and lose it all
or summon the will to scream.

I howled. A shrill, primitive wail of undiluted anger and resentment.

You responded with unexpected warmth and comfort,
brushing the soil from my battered wings,
and promising to love all the fragments of me
as we jointly try to fuse them solid, to heal the scars—
as you give me permission to pilot these hopes to the stars.

The wishes may never come true,
but they meant nothing at all without you.

If I had the self-assurance
to share my needs
from day one,
if I'd given you the chance
to let your love grow
beyond my limits,
where would we be today?
Maybe so much further,
but maybe much less strong.
There must be a reason
that it took me so incredibly long.

Finally as we take flight, hesitantly but with love,
compromise, and a spirit of unselfish giving—
I know you love the hungry soul inside of me,
the one without the confidence
to feel good enough
on the ground.

And within that love,
I feel good enough,
whether I fall or fly.

Kelley Ann Hornyak

HOPE PERSONIFIED

Dedicated to The Honorable Barack Obama

When nothing seemed impossible, we took hope for granted.
Free to laugh, to sing, to explore a world where boundaries did not exist.

History dictates that life's pattern is cyclical,
that depression follows elevation,
but that expansion also follows decrease.

The delicate balance—the ebb and flow
of ideas, of assets, of time.
These waves of change are so much
like the oceans that surround our nations,
isolating us and connecting us at the very same time.

Faith presides and reminds us
that we need to witness the destruction
to understand and appreciate the beauty of rebuilding.

A catastrophic era has ended.
A leaderless nation found rock bottom
and decided not to drown.

What could have been slow, wounded strokes to the surface
will be strong surges toward the sunlight
because a model of wisdom and integrity
has come to lead the way.
He lends strength to our broken spirits,
and deep belief that we can heal.

We will again earn the comfort we once failed to appreciate,
but this time our foundation must be a truer set of ideals.
To be an example, we must act with dignity.
We look to our president and emulate his ways.
We reach to retrieve the hope of yesterday.

CLOSER TO THE CALM

mirror balls and silver crosses dangle beneath a pure white rose
while I sit within myself, imaginary black pen in my imaginary hand
spilling words that leaked through centuries into this cup I'm drinking from
faces flash past like whipped whistling wind as I dangerously stretch
between myself and my guarded fictional past
to taste for once, the truth

of course I've never been any good at this, these guessing games
of breaking hearts and falling tears, confusion does not sift well
through worn garments like the ones I cherish even as they unravel on me
but I've been chained to this chair and this desk since the day I left
and I haven't found those answers yet
they're in the secret drawer

control is elusive on this planet, so I'll stop reaching for the reins
and flow with advice and signs and all the things I have sidestepped
every day I'll get a little closer to the calm and a little further from the storm
and I'll carry all of this with me, slowly, learning and teaching
by simply being, and loving the silence as I'm healing
and finally I'll have patience and peace

DOWNPOUR

I'm sleeping on sheets
   sewn from your tobacco-colored hair.
The midsummer breeze, watery and airless,
    ruffles billowy curtains. Abrupt, it startles
  and wakens me.

I sip liquid with intent to cool my weary body,
  but I keep choosing the glass that's filled with stale tears.
 My lofty hollow is awash with photographs and memories
   but they fail to comfort me.
  At times they disturb. They prevent me from peace.
    Tonight they prevent me from sleep.

I would cradle myself but these arms are not yours.
  They lack the warm spice that defines you and ignites me.
 Instead I ask for my eyelids to close, for dreams
    to erase the ache that broke in
 and made its sad home in my head.

One wish comes true.
  The other dies in the humid night.

I fall asleep empty and old.

Kelley Ann Hornyak

LOVING THE BROKEN HALF OF ME

I hope you keep in mind
when you're screaming at me
that I am still a broken little girl,
that my inner world has not grown,
has not changed, is still in infinite pain.

I hope you remember this
when we're careening down
those too familiar avenues,
when it all falls apart.

Because this time may be the last time—
this time may be the thing that saves us.
It may be the thing that breaks us.
But we have to take that chance,
or we will break anyway.

I love you far too much
to let you love
a broken half of me.

If you are the one,
you will get
every bit—
but I ask for your patience
while I find it.

MORNING CAME WITHOUT YOU

In loving memory of Shirley Ann Mendez (1962–2003)

I never really wrote about your loss.
Somehow I could never find the words.
I never held you close enough
to understand the way I felt
when you were gone.

I tried to be the brick walls
surrounding the ones who loved you,
encircling them and keeping out chill winds
as they huddled in tears, unable to speak.

I attempted to fill the roles I was cast for.
I tried to pour myself without ego
into their empty cups—
to simply be whatever was needed,
no questions asked and no debt recorded.

I hope I did my job as well
as God must have wanted me to.
It kept me busy while your family
was busy losing you.

Then
morning came
without you.

It was as if we had lost you twice,
plus multiple times over that month
as you fluttered in and out
of consciousness.

Kelley Ann Hornyak

Now we had no chance to hold your hand,
nor to whisper wishes in your ear—
to tell you that we would be all right,
though we knew it was a lie.

And surely I learned so much,
but I'd trade it all to bring you back—
though I know you deserve to fly free.

You gave me the gift of understanding,
to see what I had before it was gone.
You taught me love in your final hours—
how to stand in difficult moments,
and that bent does not mean broken.

The tears you brought to my eyes
gave me the clarity to see
what was right here all the time.
I wish you were here to see
all the good you have given me.

Alone I write,
but my words speak
for so many
who miss you.

I promise you we'll try
to move forward
with you in mind.
Every breath we take
will be built on your laughter—
on the memories of it
that echo through our lives.

HAIKU INTERLUDE: SKIN TO SKIN

Simple elegance
Skin to skin we melt the chill
By candle's soft glow

Kelley Ann Hornyak

YOUR SKY, YOUR EARTH

Do you understand how beautiful this world you created is? Do you personally feel the joy I touch when I look at your sky every day? When I sip the tea that's made from leaves from a faraway land, which grew in soil that you made moist, that was caressed by the warm sun and the cool winds, by your very breath? Do you witness the significance of all of this, and break me down into such steps of beauty too? I sense your omnipotent, omnipresent focus, and I press my gaze on you.

THE KILLER OF DREAMS

I haven't written much since we said goodbye,
and since we said hello again I've written even less.
The words form between my childhood and the now,
but they don't have the energy to make it to the page.
These few have arrived. Maybe they'll stay.

I trail the pen on the paper. I clack the keys.
But nothing is worthy of a single read.
The save button stares me down,
knowing it will get no click from me.

Some would call this writer's block,
but I know it's depression.
I'm sad and confused about an unsure future—
about a relationship that I want to save
and a self that I want to save even more.

I may not have to choose one over the other,
but it's the oxygen mask/airplane scenario.
I do have to help myself first.

I could be the ultimate martyr
and give up everything again
to salvage this love.
I'm not being asked to,
but I'm afraid I'll do it anyway.

When I fix myself, the love will flow,
and so will the words that elude me now.

Kelley Ann Hornyak

I blamed so much on the one
who was breathing in bed next to me,
sleeping fitfully then,
but who would now sleep serene.

The fault was ill-placed.
No one could have forced me to abandon anything.
I allowed those things to happen.

The killer of dreams was me.

PIONEER GLOW

Awkward moves I questioned—
wondered why those who did not reach
were the ones who tended to teach.

Realized in my solitude
that I was even more different
than I thought.

Glowing footsteps I followed—
emulated celebrated pioneers
to whom I was endeared.

Realized down those old paths
were the elusive answers
that I sought.

Kelley Ann Hornyak

THE QUIET

The quiet here in what was our home
is more disturbing than the words we say
when we're pretending that we're
handling this well.

Coming home to this absence of life,
of sound, of laughter.
There is no smile and no hug.
No one to greet when I walk in the door
except for the lonely feline
who can't understand
why you aren't coming back.

I keep turning on all the lights at night,
the bright white fluorescent glare
that I used to try and soften
with pretty lamps and
warm-colored shades.
You loved the darkness
and I wanted the light.
Now I have all the light I can stand
but no you.

I don't feel strong enough
to resist the pull of the tides,
the overwhelming urge
to run back to your arms
and find some relief.

But I know things will not change
unless I truly step away.
It may be for a year,
it may be forever.
I can't predict,
I can only listen
to my heart
and believe
that leaving
will prevent
more pain.

Kelley Ann Hornyak

ASH AND DUST

Wondering what comes after this.
After the breath has gone,
after the songs have slipped from our lungs.

We are lovers of life,
but what of it
if this is temporary?

Do the confines of space and time
limit the meaning of our life's work?

If catastrophe destroys the written record
of all that we poured our souls into,
does it still matter? Even when unknown?

I believe so. I have to.

The more loved ones I lose,
the less I fear the clammy grip of death.
I cannot see past the granite gravestones,
cannot predict what we'll see when we cross
from one life into the next,
or perhaps even into nothingness.

Still young but worn and weary,
I long to pack this life with good acts,
but at the same time not cling needlessly.

If my father and grandparents have gone,
if my idols and pioneers have passed,
then how can I resist the end?
I have no right to question it.
I am only ash and dust.

I ADORE US

This glow
is the warmth of the sun
after the unkind storm.
You are what is needed,
what is sought after,
what is craved.

The miraculous can't hold a candle
to the magic that we create
within these modest walls.

The setting is unassuming.
The performance is sacred, elysian.

I am humbled in your gleam,
illuminated in your shadow.

The tables are set. The stories are told.
The candles are extinguished.
The guests return home.

And we are left in exquisite solitude,
not as a lonely one, but as a perfectly paired two.

I adore this.
I adore us.

I am thankful that God gave us love.

NEEDED AS WE ARE

Through the liquid orb,
the tiniest word
is magnified
one hundredfold,
yet the meaning
becomes less clear
without context.

A heavy focus,
an intent grasp
on longings,
designs,
decisions,
distractions.
20/20 clarity
on the hidden
worlds of you,
but near blind
on the public
worlds of me.

I am gifted and robbed,
talented and handicapped,
conceived and killed.
All at the same time,
in the same breath,
in the same space.

Kelley Ann Hornyak

Simulcast across the waves,
a sunrise can only reach so far.
But this is live within us all,
24 hours, on demand, streaming.
Sleep or wake to the tunes
of young or old voices
on magnetic or wax devices.
Authenticity returning
on inauthentic roads.
It matters not which path it takes,
only that it gets there.

And the protagonist is glad
to be alive in a time
when curative words are
a required balm
for old third-degree burns
that never healed
and never will.

To be needed
as we are,
to know our role
and to fill it,
is in itself
the reason
and the meaning
that we seek.

THE MIRROR IMAGE OF THE WISTFUL STAR

A single star hangs in the center
of this morning's rose and lilac sky.
I stand, transfixed, unable to breathe,
struck by its beauty
but even more by its meaning.

The low grey clouds curl around it,
looking much like incense smoke
rising in tendrils to a higher place.
There is no one else here to witness this.
I am the mirror image of the wistful star.

Much later, in the absence of daylight,
I stand beneath the celestial sequin.
Though now joined by hundreds more,
it still glimmers more brilliantly
than any other that graces the night.

These bits of heaven can never travel and touch.
No two can ever occupy the same space,
but their candescence cannot be repressed.
Unclouded, they will fill the sky and light the earth.
It is lovely yet lonely work.

Wrapping my worn cloak of reclusion
around chilly shoulders illuminated by the moon,
at last I understand that some soul space
can never be joined together with a lover.
But letting the gleam tumble forth unburdened
is the song of love itself.

Kelley Ann Hornyak

RELIVING

Why do I keep reliving
that morning in my mind?
The ambulance, the waiting room,
saying goodbye to a body, not you.

Feeling a loved one repel my touch,
then embracing another
that I've missed so much.

A contrast of death
and life newly born,
vacant faces of nurses,
your clothes trashed and torn.

Bruises, confusion.
Together, alone.
One moment a baby,
the next I am grown.

Why is this what's on tonight,
instead of how we spent your life?

A movie of pain,
I rewind and press play.
Every night.
Every day.

SKYSCRAPER

Begin at the hidden but unchallenged root
of the infinite cravings and exquisite knowledge,
where the branched origins dig deep into the earth.
Expose the throbbing, thirsting, downward-reaching spines
that traverse through nutrient-rich dirt
and weave through watery underground springs
where mermaids play girlish games and sing.
These regions are your creative source,
but not even close to the origin of origins.
They drink their energy from the core of the planet,
which pulses with life from places we cannot see.
Still, dig as deep as you can. Begin to understand.

Lift your attention to the growth above ground,
conscious of the wooden tendrils that twist above the clouds,
the bold branches and delicate budded tips that touch heaven.
Light the swaying yet so-strong treetop with your mind.
Feel it surge with bass and beats that shake the skies.
Hear the wind whistle through and sing with soaring strings.
Sense laughter in the leaves when fairies flirt with flower kings.
This is where you catch the willing melodies,
where the lyrics tangle themselves in dreamcatchers for you.
They need no trickery, they exist to fall for you
like you once did for the tallest trees with the deepest roots.
What you see now that you couldn't then:
One of those skyscraping redwoods is you.

Kelley Ann Hornyak

THE MESSENGERS

Every message is met with abrasion,
society's rejection, or outright derision.
Each movement is countered with resistance,
each stroke of good
painted over with bad
until the villain's anger fades into indifference,
and the most persistent painter
swipes over the last bit of graffiti
with his meant-to-be victorious brush.

There is no mark on the instrument—
no plaque to state that this artist is the one.
If a clue exists, it's concealed where human eyes can't see.
Even the untouchable begins so humble,
with the key in his hands but no lock in sight.
We're created specifically
to decode the riddle,
to paint the poem,
to build the song.
It is that complex and that simple.
If we had foresight we'd never need faith.
The days and the breaths would be
taken for granted, and ultimately wasted.

We can see our own crowns if we close our eyes
and open up the honest vision that resides inside our minds.
The understanding that we're all kings and queens
doesn't lessen the special status,
except for the small-minded
and the scarcity-oriented.
It overflows. It never ends. It is within.
You don't chase—you don't strive.
You accept.
You rise.

2010

TORN SKY

The sky is torn and no one else realizes it.
Contrary to its immortal elegance,
an ill-shapen gash has made its appearance
between the ninth cloud and my residence.

Dirty truth spills from the split seam.
It's clear that nothing is as it's been.

Where summer sun once happily blinded me,
in dimness I now see disfigured beings.
I see the snakelike ugliness behind smiles—
smell the rot of death beneath these lives.

Betrayal tumbles with the acid rain.
No friend or lover will be the same.

The appraisals arrive on the angry wind.
They don't know I've heard—I'm silently singed.
I bathe in the dust, drink the sand, inhale the dusk.
I lose my sleep, surrender my health, rescind my trust.

Damage is lasting for the sky and this child.
The sun will still attempt to kill this cold.

Kelley Ann Hornyak

WHILE SHE SLEEPS

I can dance down here among the leaves—
dart between the sun-scorched blades
some distance from the sea.

She'll never see me.

I can make a haven from sticks and string,
sewn with seashells and cranberries
like jewels on a rich canopy.

Here, I dream safely.

Tucked in the brush, I am unseen,
while I turn fantasies into master plans
to lead the rest to harmony.

Someone must believe.

I can dance here on the crumpled leaves—
dart between the broken blades
too close to stormy seas.

And I will succeed
while the giant sleeps.
I'll defy her wishes for me.

TO STAND BARE

You are moist, dewy, shining like the sun.
Skin clean and free of foundations, powders,
concealers, bronzers—nothing to mask
the essential glow from within.
I noticed this long ago but I feared it.
I didn't have the confidence
to stand bare like you.
You don't swim with the school of fashion,
content in your nonconformity,
clueless as to how beautiful you are.
I admire you, the finished product.
I stand at your door,
wrapped in garments
a little too similar
to all the rest.
My shine is blotted out,
my lips an unnatural hue.
My eyelids glimmer disgustingly.
This is what I'm hiding beneath.

Kelley Ann Hornyak

YOU WANTED ME TO FEEL MY OWN JOY

This morning,
returning early to the wooded trails
I used to walk with you.
The mighty trees still sway,
the autumn leaves still whoosh,
the gravel still crunches underfoot.

I feel more like myself now
than I have in years prior.
I know myself better,
and I see just how shaped
I am by your presence
and absence.

When we first wove our way
through this maze of nature's artwork,
I was damaged and in denial.
I worked hard to handle
the immense loss
that soaked my
atmosphere.

No one,
not a soul,
heard my pain.

I wailed silently
and mourned stealthily,
with odd rituals
that over time
eased my loneliness.
Crowds and company
couldn't crack this.
I had to fix it from within.

You were steadfast in your wisdom,
having dived headlong into your faith
so many eons ago.
You disliked my vices
but believed I'd overcome them one day.
You didn't rush me.

Your desire for me to achieve
and to really live was never selfish.
Others wanted to feel their own pride.
You wanted me to feel my own joy.

Now I mourn you,
as you've flown from these trails
like the snow that melts overnight.
Life's ravaging will never dissipate,
increasing every day,
but I'm now adequately equipped
to take punches that once would slay me.

I am better for having
beaten a path with you,
once in this chaotic lifetime.

2011

THIS LOVE IS GREATER

I conceptualized a lover.
Someone unselfish, without conditions.
And someone who would put

no limits on love,
no limits on giving,

but sharp limits on the pain
that the outside world
would be allowed
to impose on me.

Someone who would enforce those boundaries,
who would protect me from the frightening things

that I decided were my enemies.

It wouldn't matter if I made sense.
It wouldn't matter if those things
would never really hurt me.

It would only matter that I believed they could,

and you would slay what I saw as dragons
even if they were created in my imagination.

I've come to accept,
grudgingly,

emptily,

that you will not be
that knight for me.

You'll only unsheathe your sword
if and when I can prove
that the dragon exists,
that it's after me,
and that the fire it breathes
can really scorch my reality.

It doesn't matter to you
if the flames only singe my dreams.

You believe I should be stronger against these things.

And still I love you.

I respect your groundedness.
I suspect that your reality
is less tangible than my fantasy,
but I believe one day we'll see eye to eye.
I'll understand the laws of the land
and you'll comprehend the power of the mind.

Until then, we'll reside in the interim,
in love's shadowy twilight,
somewhere between the lines,
and in those wrinkles etched in time.

You cannot be the vision I gave birth to.
I cannot be the person you'd like me to.

But would you mind if I stayed anyway?
Would you mind if I chose you
above all the others,
even above the fabled hero
who only exists in fairy tales?

Because to me, this love is greater.
It is real. It hurts because it's alive.
We argue our positions because we care,
and because we matter to each other.

And we may be so stubborn,
we may guard our opinions
with knives and guns and greed,
with jousts and swords and steeds,
but we're willing to die

for love,

aren't we?

Kelley Ann Hornyak

100 PROOF

Each grab of this substance,
each inhalation, each injection,
each sip, each taste,
each take is a cry for help.
It's a pitiful attempt to numb the pain,
or to placate the whiny bitch inside
that won't stop berating me
for neglecting her dreams.

I'm throwing quarters and nickels
at someone to whom I owe
several million dollars.

The more I indulge,
the more I feed the problem
that I'm trying to run from.
Large, looming, it chases me in waking hours.

The only respite I achieve is in dreams.
I can take a breath and exist freely there,
glancing in the mirror to see
that I'm exactly who I ought to be.

Then I wake. I always wake.
And the addiction strangles me.

The naive speck of yesterday—
the child I used to be—
believed she held the reins.
I'd have bet it all
on the fact (in my mind)
that I was the conductor
gripping that baton.

I controlled nothing.
I still control nothing.
I am profoundly out of control.

If becoming an adult
means making those tough decisions
and following through even when it's painful,
what does that say of my avoidance?
What does the avoidance say about me?

Some truths are lies I tell myself.
Others have always been 100-proof reality
and could never be interpreted otherwise.
The fear is where they meet.
The addiction is what they breed.

Today I understand and accept
that the longer I drug myself,
the longer I will hate myself.
The longer I try to disappear into this night,
the longer the sun will try to shine.
It won't go away. I won't die even if I want to.

Kelley Ann Hornyak

And if I do die, my guilts and regret
will only spread to those around me.
And I would never, ever
want them to become
as damaged, as destroyed,
as I am inside.

Rock bottom has become too comfortable.
I'm pushing off and chasing the pain,
my atrophied muscles burning as I swim,
bloodshot eyes squinting in unfiltered sun.

You'll be there when I break the surface.
You'll tell me I've taken too long.
You'll tell me you can't afford to believe in me again.
But you'll tell me those things whether I stay intoxicated
or whether I straighten out and stay that way.

I still don't hold the reins.
I'll never hold the reins.
But I choose to be lucid.
I choose the pain.
I choose to wake.

2014

ILLEGAL ALIEN/PEARLS BEFORE SWINE

I was a weak thing, a child of not much confidence.
I wanted so badly to learn a thing or two.
To learn everything, really, between the earth and the moon.
I knew my dreams were safe within the confines of my own breast,
like the heart, meant to be hidden,
beating hard but shielded
from light, air, and human stares.
I felt so fragile. I was so strong.
So quiet but so full of song.

But you see, when I felt loved and safe,
I still knew to protect my gifts
beneath my wings.
Later when I learned that love was not for me,
that unconditional was a conditional dream,
I cut open my ribs and I let that beast sing,
and the monsters bludgeoned that love-starved thing.

Pearls before swine.
But no one taught me these things.

I was sheltered and/or spoiled
depending on who you talk to.
In fact, those are compliments
compared to the venom they now spew.
But I wouldn't trade that innocence
for their prepubescent jadedness
or their slow descent into madness.

Kelley Ann Hornyak

I'm a bit more street smart, yes.
But I will not bend
or consent
to citizenship in their world.
I am an illegal alien,
a temporary traveler,
just passing through
to learn that thing or two
between the earth and the moon.

CANYONS

My chasms are the lines in fingerprints,
microscopic and often mocked
by those who cross canyons
and cannot relate or compare.

They peer in from a safe distance,
sometimes squinting from many miles,
often reminiscing and guessing
from many moons or many rooms or many tombs.

They sink their fangs into zero truth—
they cling to conjecture and rumors.

This used to bother me so.
I used to scream within and without,
struggling to be understood and accepted.
Today, I observe. I contemplate but don't care.
I'm immune to the judgment and stares.

Kelley Ann Hornyak

AS IS

Nightmares still rip me from the comfort that could be sleep,
turning comfortable well-lit spaces into dark wells of hatred.
In those unconscious hours, your dream form chases me
through gardens of weeds and hoarded useless things.
She traverses it all with ease and murders me.

Not verbal accusations like in the waking world,
but physical destruction. The end of me.
You couldn't be more bloodthirsty.

Still, in those dreams, I try to reason with you.
I hold back the knife as you stab at my chest—
I remind you of a time when your ill will was less.
While awake, I'm clear and comfortable with all that I know.
While asleep, I'm confused and still struggling to let go.

As much as I work to wipe away the stain,
my gut tells me that these visions will continue to haunt me—
will worsen as the years pass and as the loss becomes mine.
Because you are just fine with broken connections and burnt bridges.
I am the only child who still plays connect the dots
and who isn't satisfied with puzzles unfinished.

But short of an intervention, I can't fix this.
And even then, it would be falseness.
I must accept that you're just the tragedy that bears the gift
of knowing that I am good enough as is.

THE GOOD PATIENT

The fear of doing the wrong thing
is greater than that of doing nothing.
When doctors are just guessing
and throwing drugs at my pain,
all I can see is time ticking by
with dangerous assumptions being made.

I try to be the good patient,
but am I throwing breaths and heartbeats away?
Am I losing years and months and days?
I am so afraid.

So much technology is within reach.
I'm now insured but it's withheld from me.
Wouldn't want to waste a dollar
on diagnostics to be sure.
Just write a prescription,
remind me I'm young
and that I look healthy,
so I must be healthy.
I worry too much and
the hurt means nothing.
Go home and stop complaining.

RELIEF

Relief comes in stutters.
Smooth seas between
rough waves.

I am parched
but cannot drink
this tease
that's smashing
at my face.

The land winks
in short glimpses
betwixt the siren's bray
and the storm's rain.

I see the future.
I feel my faith.

I hold on
and I steer
and I pray.

SIMPLE SOLUTION

A simple solution is presented without fanfare.

A hint of not-so-difficult on the horizon,
a whisper of could-be-simple at the door.
Perhaps I have been overthinking it all—
ruminating on everything that could go wrong
instead of recognizing everything that has gone right.

I want to research—instead I just try.

For now, it seems to work—seems to solve the riddle.
There's a calmness and a feeling of nourishment.
My body and my soul seem in-sync and in-tune.
Placebo or proof? Time always tells.
For now, I'll relax into the still and quiet night.

The struggle is removed and I'm feeling fine.

Kelley Ann Hornyak

UNTIL THEY FORGOT

Returning that fall to the cage
after a summer away—
the summer when everything changed.

A sick, hungry buzz in the air—
questions flying like bullets,
assumptions made without care.

They didn't ask me.
Didn't know we shared a block—
didn't know I knew the truth.

I buried my face in a book
until they forgot about you.

THE HOPEFUL PLACE

Spring comes rushing in on the winds.
I feel it in my bones and on my skin—
feel the breeze chase away the hurt in my knees
and the brokenness in my heart.

I turn my face to the sun
and try to trust,
but I have learned
not to rely on
what seems to be
good or sweet.
A simple gust can
sweep it all from me.

I'm just beginning to find my footing
after the hardest fall of my life.
Recovery was unexpected
and all I want is for it to stay.
This year has been so good to me.
Will the rest of it continue to be?

I look back over the three previous years
of physical pain and mental confusion,
when I questioned my life's meaning
and the longevity for which I was reaching.
I see now the possibility for love and life to continue.
I see that I may be one of the lucky ones
or I may be not at all.

Kelley Ann Hornyak

No guarantees,
but hope itself
is delectably sweet
right now.

I cling to the warmth,
chase the wings on the winds,
and burrow into the
feathered hopeful place
where I feel safe.

HAIKU INTERLUDE: TSUNAMI DREAMS

Tragic dreams haunt me
Tsunamis bear down on us
Tell that life's fleeting

Kelley Ann Hornyak

WHO YOU'LL BE APART

Human hearts are far too flawed

to handle the gift of love.

We attempt the task ourselves each day

but we know that we're ill-equipped.

At least we've got the benefit of years behind us

to strengthen our resolve

and give us confidence in each other.

I can't imagine starting fresh, like you tried to do.

Trying to solidify something so free-flowing —

forging paper contracts from the love letters of the soul —

reigning in the natural tendencies of songbirds who love to soar.

Watching these two beautiful spirits give up and let go

is a sad moment for two who loved flying with you —

who were inspired by you —

who will miss you.

A eulogy for who you were together,

with hope and love for who you'll be apart.

Kelley Ann Hornyak

THE SPEED OF LIFE

Those years of my life
looked much like
time-lapse city photography,
cars rushing by
just a blur
of neon lines,
daylight turning to nighttime
in the blink of an eye.

Without warning,
the scene slows
to the speed of life.

The cars regain lines,
headlights, and tail lights.
They freeze at the stop signs.
I can see the people within
and they are very much alive.
They are talking and laughing,
playing with the radio dial
and checking on kids in the backseat.

There are artists on street corners
selling their work or singing their songs.
There are smiles on their faces
though these are tough times,
and passersby appreciate their gifts,
leaving a token of thanks
and a well-wish.

No longer time-lapse,
not even photography,
life is now real and tangible for me.
I move from observing
to being a part of the scene.
It's not a game—not a race.
I have a say. I have a place.

Kelley Ann Hornyak

RECOLLECTIONS/DESTINY ON FIRE

We walk through doors and into shops
that have had so many incarnations
as the times have changed.
I have had eons of recollections
just sitting right here waiting
and now I have recollections
of those recollections
and on and on
and on.

I have aged
as surely as they said I would
and I have had regrets
but fewer than they predicted.

Those of us who are lost in our heads,
who cruise down mostly cerebral avenues
make less life-shaking mistakes
because we know ourselves so well
and we know before it happens
that it's going to hurt like hell.
We know when it is worth it
and when it's best to stay in our shells.

A familiar song comes on in this shop
and the vibes of salt lamps and incense
make me receptive to the lyrics and message.
The time in which it was a hit
was one of potential, of reflectiveness,
and I miss it.
I miss that moment of pause
when a few different decisions
would have solved things that much sooner.
When the world was on that glimmering platter
and I could shake some sense into myself
to make it matter.

But here we are.
We made it anyway.
Smiles flit between our faces
and love flies between us.
We are sometimes broken and tired,
but not tonight.
Tonight we are a memory in the making.
Tonight we are destiny on fire.

Kelley Ann Hornyak

NOVEMBER-HEARTED

This spring walk feels like summertime
and I am coming back to life.
Iced coffee chases the heat away
but I drink in the humidity
and I want it to stay.
It curls my hair
and makes my skin moist
and I want you to kiss me
and feel my need for you.

But you are a child of autumn
and can't wait for the leaves to fall.
This weather does not thrill you
and there are too many other
spring-fevered love seekers
stealing space at this park.
The bees are already competing
with me for your attention,
buzzing through your hair
and causing a stir.

No, this isn't the time or place
to woo a November-hearted girl.

HAIKU INTERLUDE: BLOOD MOON

Beneath the blood moon
We bathe, ocean's burgundy
Eclipse hints at end

Kelley Ann Hornyak

BLED

You'll never know what you lost,
and that's more than okay.
It's better that way.
You don't need more pain
and I don't need to bathe
in the bittersweet memories
that are all I have left.
I don't need to live
in a space of regret
because I know without question
that I did what I needed to do.
I opened my wounds.
I spoke my truth.
I bled all over you.

10,000 NIGHTS

It's beneficial that you don't know
the healing storm of beauty you let go.
You would cry 10,000 nights of black tears,
losing sleep in the soundlessness—
losing sanity in the solitude.
Your ears would long for my lullabies
while your heart drowned in our goodbyes.
Your hunger would compare my embodied steam—
this luscious physical cornucopia of dreams—
with her meager and ordinary offerings.
You would backtrack and regret the past,
wishing you had just done this or said that.
You would press on through countless hard workdays,
sweating out the pain of watching me fade.
You would pour your dollars
into mind-numbing substances,
attempting to drink and smoke my image away
but actually searing it in deeper,
branding my name
or tattooing my stain
into a face already so strained.
But no, you don't know all that's within me.
You'll never comprehend all that you set free.
You'll continue on your trek and live boldly.
You'll never realize the blessings you spent.
We'll both find bliss in your ignorance.

Kelley Ann Hornyak

THE SEA-DWELLER AND THE EARTH-BOUND

This legged creature hates the mermaid
that reawakens inside her every spring.
She hates her because the sea-dweller
is a feminist and a woman of confidence.
The earth-bound one is downtrodden
and more than happy to remain that way.
She finds it easier to drown her desires than to fight the system.
But every time the ocean warms and the hibiscus begins to bloom,
that insatiable inner being smirks and plots and schemes,
turning the complacent into a miserable and stubborn thing.

One masks her love as hatred and buries her emotion under ice,
but the other, her Gemini, won't comply, splashing sun-warmed saltwater
to thaw and melt the numbness from her atrophied limbs and heart.
She fights hard against efforts that should be appreciated—
flings hurt and hurls daggers at delicate fins.
She can't imagine that the siren goddess might win.

All that the mermaid wants is for both to swim, sing, and play—
for these once indistinct personalities to again blend and integrate.
She doesn't seek to destroy the life that's been built or to take anything away.
And she is filled with empathy,
understanding why the legged one is so jaded—
why she's so filled with fear, unable to entertain a seemingly silly sea-maid.

These two archenemies pulled from one personality might battle into eternity.
Fairy tales scream for happy endings but fate and time always have their say.
It's undetermined how the story will end and which femme fatale will prevail.
But I'll tell you a secret. I'm rooting for the one with the tail.

THE BABY, THE BATHWATER

The baby. The bathwater.
That old trope.
But I was a teenager
and hearing it for the very first time.
I understood that the baby was the knowledge
and the bathwater was the bullshit
but I didn't want to be in that prison
no matter what metaphors my mentor spun.

I longed to tell her that I was the baby
and the bathwater was poisoned.

What I'd yet to see
was that I was as alive as I would ever be.
I was still inspired, still excited, still breathing.
There are days I can no longer claim all three.

Regardless, I'm clawing, clamoring at a rebirth.
I'm digging through those memories
to ensure that I don't trip over the same mistakes.
That I don't let the status quo
determine what's next for my soul.

And if I could,
I'd go back to that moment—
the baby, the bathwater—
and throw everything away
but me.

WELCOME

This feels good.
This, right here.

Chosen family.

There's a welcome sign on the door
and it's not just for decor.

Laughter rings
and it's with,
not at.

Not everyone shares blood
but it's clear that we share love.

We feel safe.
We feel wanted.

When one hurts,
we all hurt.
When one feels joy,
we all celebrate.

The circle is open
and never broken.

This is where I always should have been.

THE MOMENT OF MARRIAGE

I never thought that love would be a blessing I could count.
I never believed that another human being would mesh with me.
When you came into my world, I didn't know how to behave.
I cowered from all your affection and turned you away.
I'm sorry today.

I look back on the greatest and most understated reunion of my life,
when you and I touched truth and decided we could not sever ties.
I wax poetic on this, because for me, it was salve on every wound.
It was the healing I sought everywhere but where I should have.
I was blind to the bounty that you laid in front of me,
and the realization of your love was the grace that saved me.

Like the fables etched in time,
you and I have become an immeasurable entity.
Mythical, it seems we should be.
Yet we're flesh and blood and breathing.
Still nothing can come in between.

Should the fire reach our door,
I'll sweep you up and carry you away
to the place where love rains every day—
where destructive flames cannot burn,
and irrelevant becomes the outside world.

Kelley Ann Hornyak

Boldly, I'll say—their theories hold no sway.
Interlocked souls may stretch but never part.
The moment of marriage
is not within an intricately planned ceremony.
It is a spontaneous spell
that turns intertwined fingers
into intermixed spirits.
No separation can occur.

I will fight for you
should any suitor mistakenly dream
that they have the power to interfere.

There exists no device that can rip apart what we've sewn—
not starry-eyed minstrels who sing you love lyrics,
not overarching indifference gathered from dry decades,
not even death with its finality and stealthy ways.

Whatever comes next, we'll conquer it.
Wherever we go with our last breaths, we'll reunite there yet again.
Even all the darker times and question marks will make sense.
Up there on the trophy shelf with our victory plaques
will be the snapshots and memories of the challenging half—
of the battles we fought and won, and of the tears we shed for love.

I wouldn't trade a heartbeat of it for calmer seas
because without those times I wouldn't know
how far I'd go for you or how far you'd go for me.
I celebrate it all today. The sun, the storms, the everything.

I wake up every morning knowing that I am complete.
That I've found the one whose jagged edges fit with mine,
so that we seem smooth and clean and unbroken
under all but the most high-definition scrutiny.

This union, this marriage, this bond—
it needs no formal recognition to make it real and permanent.
The papers the others are approved to sign
get torn in two and tossed in the fire.
If the earthly rulers grant us that status,
we'll use it as a license to uplift one another.
But signatures and circles of gold are transitory.
Our names were carved out of the sky in stars
before our cries hit the air at the moments we were born.
We are the destiny that divinity has spun. We are already one.

Kelley Ann Hornyak

HAIKU INTERLUDE: VISIONARIES

Wondering, muted
How brilliant visionaries
Give up normalcy

BANSHEES

What I must look like from the outside.
I can almost understand
the banshees that scream against us.

All they see is my drowned potential,
my blighted spirit,
my spiraling downfall.
They look for a scapegoat,
as even I sometimes do.

All eyes, like daggers, on you.

But what I deny
and what they don't see
is that nobody is responsible for me
but me.

And if anyone is,
maybe they should be,
because they were the ones
depicted as guides.
They were the ones
who could have rightfully advised.

But they chose to step aside.

Kelley Ann Hornyak

So this is my province,
my charge and my duty.
If I fail or succeed,
make no mistake,
it's on me.

The wasted time
was almost endless
but filled with lessons,
and I'm more prepared now
than they dream I must be.

What I look like is not who I am
and my fate remains in my hands.

ALL FALLS TOGETHER

Looking back over the scattered papers
twisted and crumpled on the master bedroom floor,
I see how a line from 1989 fits with one from 2004—
how another from '92 blends with one from the present year,
and so on and so on and so on,
page after page after page.

The seemingly disconnected words
become poetic puzzle pieces
and life reveals itself to be anything but random.
The days I divorced myself from
become cherished memories
and I'm anything but bitter
as I recall broken hearts
and dead-end dreams.

This once cavernous dressing chamber
has become just a room like any other,
yet the magic is still in the structure,
still coursing life through the beams.
So much has been gutted and altered,
but no one has rewired the electricity
and nothing can rewrite the original meaning.
The destruction was an illusion.
The creator never left the scene.

Kelley Ann Hornyak

The pages dance back into place,
straightened, with newly gilded edges,
opulence spilling over from expensive inks.
The writings of a mad woman
have transformed into art at its finest,
tales of lives lived,
of loves loved,
of losses left
for a fresh start
without confusion
about what it all means
and who deserves to share it with me.

The dreamer and the artist are finally fused,
as are the procrastinator and the overachiever,
the killer and the muse.

ANIMALS

We are animals, unevolved.
Perched on opposite viewpoints,
flinging rocks at love's face.

How could we skillfully craft these monuments
only to smash them to rubble?

We looked down on others
for doing the same.
Maybe this is karma.
Maybe we've just changed.

But isn't there a silver thread
above it all
that keeps us connected,
that keeps our bond solid,
that cannot be severed?

And won't it save us this time?

Kelley Ann Hornyak

HAIKU INTERLUDE: NOTHING TO SAY

Nothing to say now
We fill up the silence with
Black sky, winking stars

TRAVELOGUE

The pitter-patter of the footsteps of the past
won't stop tapping in my ears tonight.
It's soft, muted, padding it's way
through the more traveled parts of my mind,
but it's incessant and unbending in its purpose.
I don't mind it. I need its courage.

If the present is to be a healing parade
and I'm to wake up each day
with a scoop of hope on my plate,
then there's no time to believe in anything less
than the concept that everything else has been a test.

When the future's finest flies through my open door
and the pain that birthed my body of work
doesn't exist in my heart and soul anymore,
what will be left of me
will be what I was meant to be.
What I was made to be.
Empty of all falsity and fiction,
bare of all the lies they fed to me.

Kelley Ann Hornyak

ALL THE WHILE FREE

Victimized and terrified, I saw the world above me disappear
as I spiraled down endlessly into the empty cavern they crafted.
The cavern that I funded, that I drew blueprints for and constructed.
I blamed them time and time again for imprisoning me within it—
all the while standing beside it, free as I could ever be,
believing I was gone so deep
that no one could save me.

You looked on so helplessly.
How could you save the child who resisted saving?
And a child I remained, though the years did not spare me.
Confused inside, I questioned why—
why their words burned and left such lasting scars,
why I could not blend in instead of being their mark,
why I spent my life so bruised, battered, and marred.
All the while free, all the while free.
I could always step away.
I could always love me.

Where I saw muddied and broken wings,
I now see such wondrous things.
I see my thoughts and vision
can change those disabled appendages
into hands that reach and skin that feels,
into fingers that mold the external
into a golden gift that validates the soul.

Humbled yet empowered,
I realize that I was not given this life
to let them tread on me
or to stay stuck in those memories
that become amplified and more real with time.
When cold, when hurting, when jaded, when empty,
I now say please and ask for healing.
I do not want to end as bitter as I began.
I dip my mind into the waters of wholeness.
I will learn how to dream again.

Kelley Ann Hornyak

DIAGNOSIS: WRONG

I had the symptoms—
they made assumptions.

I settled for a quarter of a diagnosis
that I felt three-quarters sure of
and it turned out it wasn't worth a quarter
or a nickel or a penny
or a thought.

I've been a part of you—
a part of this community—
connecting through our shared suffering
but staying at a safe distance
because I knew the doctors might be wrong
and I might have to leave you.

And leave I must.
I don't belong.
The diagnosis was wrong.

Who wouldn't love to hear that?
To run like the wind away from it?
And I do. I run from it—from you.
I feel guilty and ashamed
as I dust off my wings,
not broken after all,
just underused.

A little therapy just might heal me
while you are left with no cause or cure.
How cruel of nature. How unjust—unfair.

Call me what you like.
Blessed or just fortunate.
But know that I'm not ungrateful
and that I wish you were lucky too.

I fly but my ears still ring of you.
My soul is still pained when you hurt.
When you whirl out of control
and your world feels so small,
I long to land within it and
make it sturdy,
make it solid,
make it stop.

Maybe I can still make a difference
though I've flown the coop.
Maybe my freedom will give me a voice
that I wouldn't have had if I shared your disease.
I could never speak for you
but I have learned a thing or two
and if you'd like an ally, here I am.

RESTORATION COMPLETE

Creativity reawakened,
slumber interrupted,
hibernation over.

With well-placed words,
I denounce depression.
I decry public opinion—
still defy expectation.

With daily work,
I push through blocks,
I heal the hurt,
I change my world.

With open heart,
I steal the sky,
I drink the ocean,
I move the mountains.

Intentions reinstated,
assailants intercepted,
restoration complete.

HAIKU INTERLUDE: GARDENS OF DREAMS

For love, I believe
Watered gardens of dreams will
Return you to me

Kelley Ann Hornyak

8-BIT

I can feel that button pressing—
my life resetting.
Though you left me,
I will carry the echoes
of the things I thought
I loved about you,
whether or not true.
I will cherish
the ghost coins
that disappear
in my hands,
leaving me broke
and grasping.
Why? To my mind,
they are as real
as the desert hill's sunshine
or the iced land's snow
and I can't imagine
this 8-bit life
without those.

Who would I be
if I let this battle
make me as bitter
and damaged as you?
Some would say
that you'd have won.
I would say
we'd both have lost.
This is only a game
and there's no glory
no matter how
it turns out now.
The system is obsolete
and the cartridge is
lost in a trash heap.
Only memories,
only memories.

The best that I can do
is to play the sequels
exactly as they come,
whether with friends
or happily alone—
whether with pink wings
or swimming down below.
I'll look for
the moments—
the memories—
not the score.
And if I save the princess,
this time I'll love her more.

Kelley Ann Hornyak

Decades on,
the boss is inconsequential.
It really is about the journey.
One day I may even realize
that I am the hero, villain, and victim—
the programmer and the creative director.
Not narcissistically, but truthfully,
in hindsight it comes down
to loving me
in pixels, in 3D, or in reality.

ALCHEMISTS

I want us to fall madly in love with each other,
once again, like we were way back when.
One dream, one fantasy, one hope for the future—
just to ravish and be ravished in return.

Part of falling together is drifting gently apart
as the years and the tides do their dirty work,
the waves washing away sand and rock,
morphing the coastline we worked to create.

It is not destruction—it is simply change.
It is nature in her softest and most natural state.
She's not whipping up tornadoes and typhoons—
just gentle lapping of the sea by light of the moon.

We knew when we began that we would get here—
that we'd survive and be a little love-scarred.
It is much akin to battle, and perhaps better then
than when it's apathetic, neutral, and bland.

If we, as alchemists, can transmute these flames
from flickers of past pain into fires of present passion,
we can burn for decades and then turn to sultry smoke,
flitting to the heavens and kissing the stars themselves.

Like other legendary lovers who live on in ink and paper,
our immortality is in the tale, our longevity in the taper.
For the candles must burn a lifetime long for you and I to earn
our place within the ages and our lyrics within the song.

2015

GROWTH

This day feels different
than all the rest.

I wake, I work—
I do the things I've done
a thousand times before.

Rote.
Rote.
Rote.

But the routine that
has only stifled me
seems transformed—
even enlightening.

That same old effort is engulfed
by a fresh, genuine desire.

I wake, I work—
I do the things I've done
a thousand times before.

Grow.
Grow.
Grow.

Kelley Ann Hornyak

ALL THAT MATTERS

Image doesn't matter.

What they think doesn't matter.

The pain doesn't matter.

All that matters and remains
is the love we leave behind.

And I loved so greatly
even though I failed to show it.

I hope it does matter.

I hope it does remain
when I'm gone.

2016

MUSIC IN ME

Restoration,
renovation.

It's not that perfect past,
but it is what it is.

And in the midst of hugs
and conversations
with old friends,

I can see, so clearly,
the real me.

While I have been trying
to hold all the pieces together,
to keep the outside as it always was,

the inside never changed,
at least not in the ways that mattered.

I am still a lover,
a writer,
a singer,
a dreamer.

Those dreams
still have wings.

Kelley Ann Hornyak

I have stared mortality
in its unavoidable face,

and I don't know when
I will part with this reality,

but I do know I won't die
with the music in me.

A FEW WORDS

When I snap out of the haze
and actually feel like myself
for a moment,

you're still there,

no further away
than you were then.
You're still my friend.

And all the distance
and difference
in the universe

can't rearrange
what heaven has placed.

Maybe we've been touched by tragedy,
but you're still you and I'm still me,
and a few words can heal
what continues to bleed.

Kelley Ann Hornyak

THIN AIR

Covered in cobwebs—
nothing has changed.
And maybe that's why
I feel this pain.

Maybe I need to
open the windows, open the doors,
open conversations that lead to more.

Clearly, I'm healing.
My mind's on the mend.
But I wonder how is yours,
my friend?

Do you too have nightmares
instead of restful sleep?
Certain triggers, like morbid souvenirs,
that you insist you keep?
Because if you let go
and if you forgot,
you'd trade mourning the missing
for missing the mourning.
Because you and me—
who would we be
if we found that long-lost peace?

Does your back hurt from the workday
or from the past that seeps through the cracks?
Do your eyes look tired from the life you live now
or from the one that was left in the past?

All these questions, I ask of thin air
in the space where we laughed
when we could still care.

I hope time is kind
and gives us the chance
to rekindle our friendship,
to finish this dance.

This hiding,
this pining,
this lying
through our teeth.

The answers lie between us,
not in nightmares and dreams.

Kelley Ann Hornyak

ARMOR

Some seethe at my lack of anger,
but I've been angry enough for a lifetime.
I have poured decades into resentment
and smashed potential into pavement,
and I haven't got any bitterness left in me.

It matters not if you scour me with words.
My skin is that much thicker than yours.
An armor that allows for flexibility
surrounds and envelops and protects me.
You cannot hurt me. I have found my peace.

There is so much more meaning to my life
than in your uneducated appraisal of it.
I don't need your judgment or approval anymore.

And as I turn the other cheek,
and as you ask for help from me,
I'll give it freely, not emotionally.
By helping you, I'm healing me.

When I go,
I want to have let go.
When I leave,
I want to be free.

A LOT LIKE HEAVEN

It felt a lot like heaven—
those sunny, sultry days.

I remember kissing lips like clouds
in the afternoon peach haze—
the room as filled with sunlight
as we were with youth and desire.

Your body, warm.
Your scent, clean.
Your arms wrapped
around every bit of me.
Our minds on only one
and yet a billion things.

Upstairs,
upstairs,
that place of dreams.

Baring it all in broad daylight,
windows open, curtains billowing,
wind sweeping through
like I swept over you.

And we laughed
and we loved
and we hovered on the precipice
of something I truly should have embraced
if only my brain could stay in one place.

Kelley Ann Hornyak

But I second guessed
and doubled regrets
and understood
this was not a yes.

It was not a forever.
It was a for now.

But in that tiny time
in a hopefully long life,
you managed to teach me things
that I will never leave behind:

To respect and stand up for myself.
To express and not suppress myself.
To love myself and others
in both light and in dark.
To not waste my talents and gifts
on those who don't ignite from my spark.

And you didn't catch fire,
but you glowed a bit.
You were worth the trip
and I thank you for it.

ODDLANDS

Welcome to the land of odd,
where upside-down is downside-up
and questioning the answers
gets you admission to the club.

Floating on chilled clouds,
the weight of the world drops,
the pressure of time stops,
and imagination reigns.

The dreams we thought were dead and gone
are breathed back to life again.

The music—with its staccato staircases,
syncopated and synthesized—
from analog to digital, from ether to ears.
It is visual and spatial,
tangible and real.
It caresses and heals
the broken hearts
and shredded brains
and gives the thorned beasts
their courage again.

In the fields of flowers,
we find whatever we've been seeking.
Always there, beneath the blossoms and leaves,
never deliberately hidden from you or from me.

Kelley Ann Hornyak

Just waiting.
Anticipating.

Reunions,
reintegrations,
relief.

And the anger you spent
as the unknowing knave
on the well-meaning vizier,
when the wishes you wished for
were somewhere out there.

But all those tiny wounds
that have been hampering you
will now close.
You'll be whole,
your armor needed no more.

You'll remember the path of the gods
between the oddlands and the land of odd,
and you'll get more and more free
as you think more of you
and less of me.

EYES OF LOVE

Eyes of love
looking back at kismet sadness.
How can the human brain regret
what the universe has deemed to be fate?
How could the heart decide to break
when it could continue beating
for the short time we're allotted for living?

I'm a writer
so I carry my past with me
like well-worn luggage,
covered with stickers from places afar
that seem so distant—
another life among the stars.

Some hellish planets that flamed and burned—
some heavenly rings where we spun and churned.
Most in-betweens that were worth all of me.
I wasn't always present,
but from here, I'll be.

Looking back in anger?
Not me.

Kelley Ann Hornyak

HE BREAKS THE NIGHT

In loving memory of Michael Keith Prieur (1930–2016)

This moment has teeth.

The loss is piercing,
the reverberations biting.

I feel the wrinkles as they creep
and I sense the lack of distance
between my breathing and your not-being.

Imagine all the tears we shed
between point A and B.
Imagine all the fun we could have had,
just you and me.

It's all history.
All a mist of a once-possible dream.

But this is a bookend of an era,
and I embrace the strange,
for life and death themselves are change.

Farewell to this unnamed age.

ANXIETY CREEPS

Anxiety creeps
in moments of gladness,
in moments of calmness,
in moments of silence.

It steals joy,
this thief of happiness,
and leaves you questioning
the strength of the steel tethers
that connect you to the components
that make up a life well-lived.

Where you used to
sleep soundly,
you wake.
Where you would have
laughed loudly,
you cry.
Where you could have
reveled wildly,
you slink back.
You miss out,
you skip out,
you dip out.

Kelley Ann Hornyak

But you also learn the skill of resilience.
You adopt coping skills that should be instinctive.
You eventually morph from the screaming victim
into the beaming superhero who saves herself.
And along the way, you may help a few others
who are drowning in their own fears and despair,
not realizing that there's no water at all
and an abundance of fresh air.

Anxiety creeps,
but fear of the fear
is what keeps you
here instead of there.

DREAM MAKER

Dedicated with love to Janet Jackson and Eissa Al Mana

Good morning, Miss Janet.
Young love said what will be will be—
today you say you do want this to be reality.
If that wistful, wishful magic
is working its way through
your now stronger broken heart,
then let me be one of many to say
this will be your greatest work
and most divine work of art.

Two times the power
down that street of 2,300 dreams
where you waited a good long while
for time to fly and love to sing—
where your heart is not empty—
where it now is so full
that the knowledge
of the state of this lonely world
doesn't scare you away
from bringing fresh new life
into a world they didn't make.

Someday is, in fact, tonight.
If the audience beyond the curtains
is so euphoric, so excited,
then you and your LUV must be spinnin' tonight.

Kelley Ann Hornyak

If this time, this era,
throbs with a new agenda,
then boldly ask for more
simply because of love—
simply to continue that flawless line
of talented dreamers
who can change stubborn minds.

Or keep them safe behind that rope of velvet,
tucked tightly to your breast in a hug that never ends.

Better yet, give them the control
that you once had to fight for.
Let them be who they are
in a free xone of clouds and truth.

So come on, get up, and love scene till it rains—
until the theory is the truth—
until a magic hour leads to daybreak—
until a '90s love groove becomes a '10s black eagle—
until the great forever never lets you go
and you leave behind another deep mind
to lead our steps and change the times.

Dream maker, go rhythmically into that night
and know without question it's gon' B all right.
Come back to me with living diamonds
gleaming with discipline and meaning,
glowing from an island life.
Enjoy and bask in the glow of family,
whether blood, blended, or extended.

Inshallah and sweet dreams, Mama Janet,
and to the promise of you,
your baby.

NO HOME

I wake up with these songs in my head
and I wonder what they're trying to tell me
or what I'm trying to tell myself.

What am I ignoring?
What am I glossing over?
I know the answers
but my fear keeps me frozen solid,
stuck within thick blocks of ice
in a land that's always been
just a bit too slippery for me.

What if reaching for heaven
results in a fiery fall to hell?
What if every hope I've ever held
just holds me tight to tragedy?

What if every story
is just the very same one,
told over and over again,
sickly, cyclically,
until the storyteller
comprehends
their beginning
or their end?

Like clouds,
like satellites,
we zoom by
alone.

Kelley Ann Hornyak

No destination—
no home.

KNOW PEACE

The peace you took from me
is suddenly easily within reach.
My synapses fire and remind me
that it wasn't personal,
that we were young,
that we didn't know better.

That if you'd known I'd be so affected
even after decades away from the pain,
that you wouldn't have had the heart
to inflict it upon me.

That if I'd known you were in such pain yourself,
that I'd have turned the other cheek
or even reached out my hand
in empathy and friendship.

Imagine that.

And though we'll never know
what difference it may have made,
rewriting the story within my brain
gives me understanding and perspective
to let me love and trust again.

Kelley Ann Hornyak

I don't regret sharing a childhood with you.
I could label you a bully—myself, a victim.
But wouldn't that be too simplistic of a view?
Weren't we both victims of the system?
Of parental worldviews and societal pressures?
Weren't we both just children? Just kids?

Some say that I'm too forgiving,
but who drank the poison but me?
There is no revenge in resentment,
and even if there was, no peace.

You are no longer in my classroom—
no longer even in my rear-view.
So in my prayers, I wish you well.
What else is left to do?

THE WEIGHT OF YOUR WORLD

Things sure didn't turn out the way that I thought they would.
Here I am, smoking the past away, popping pills to numb the pain,
and realizing that it's time to embrace the mist of the cannabis
and kiss the pharmaceuticals goodbye.

I work in this industry
but it's killing me.
Hypocritical? Maybe.
But I can see both sides.
It's always gray—
never black, never white.

I leaned on a doctor and on a drug,
believing that they could save me from myself.
But the work that needed to be done
was on my mind and heart,
not on my body.

Yes, I did learn so much here.
Yes, I'm resolving the issues as I go.
Yes, the experience was valuable.
Yes, I'd trade it all for what was simple.

Someone once told my mother
that the real world would break me.
That she protected me too much
and that I'd never understand reality
or be able to live within it.

Kelley Ann Hornyak

30 years later, it's broken me a time or two,
but if I could sit down and talk to her,
I think she'd see my strength
through the pieces that have healed.
I used to crack like kindling,
but now I bend and snap right back.

I still live by my own rules and in my own little world,
but I'm not dying under the weight of yours.

PACIFIC

Icepick headaches—
nightmares of venomous snakes.
These are the things
that jolt me awake.

I know,
down to my soul,
that I have these unsweetened dreams
because I feel out of control.

I handle uncertainty
like a child handles patience.
I want to live forever.
I want no pain
and no frustration.

But that's not the design
of this life—this situation.

I must find calm in the storm of it.
I must create the cool in the warmth of it.
I have to channel my ancestors
who held it together
so elegantly,
no matter the weather.

Kelley Ann Hornyak

Sometimes I envy
their position
six feet beneath,
because wherever their spirits are,
they must be soaring and free.
Not trapped down here in worry,
like me.

Come and sweep through me,
pacific winds west to east.
Calm this crying baby
that still inhabits me.

WALKING AWAY SEASON

Signs flashed sharp and cold—
it was walking away season.

I cuddled up carelessly
in my old woolly blanket,
itching and scratching
and lying and laughing.

The living, breathing
landscape beckoned
just outside my
curtained panes.

The clean air and open space
looked thrilling but so scary.

Defiant, I threw a match
and the weather report
into the fireplace.

Denial was still
the coziest space
and I thought I knew
better than fate.

Kelley Ann Hornyak

HER RELIGION IS LOVE

In a Turkish teahouse,
she savors the delicate flavors
of vanilla, rose, and pomegranate—
inhales intoxicating aromas
of the richest, darkest çay
that the Black Sea Coast
has oh-so-lovingly
given birth to.

Within her own soul,
this abode of Jehovah,
of Bhagavan,
of Allah,
of Om,
she invokes her own
avatars,
deities,
and idols,
and longs for home.

In this space of Ananda,
of Nirvana,
of Zen,
she recalls distant lovers
and wishes for a friend.
That empty space,
she fills with books—
with words,
with chapters—
with choruses,
with hooks.

Awakening,
awareness—
she seeks them both
in bright sunlight
and moonless, starless blackness.

In Sri Lanka,
she dozes under a Bodhi tree,
lulled to sleep by Ceylon tea.
China brings its bountiful Buddha
and enlightenment through tea leaves green.
The noble truths bring comfort and peace
and she longs to stay,
but her heart says flee.

Kelley Ann Hornyak

Lakshmi calls gently
and she flashes silver through the skies
to India, the land of the sacred and the wise.
She visits temples, swims in seas,
drinks chai hot, creamy, and spicy—
lets go of every vestige of the ordinary.
She chants and hums in watts and ohms,
electrical as her blood and bones.
She finds peace
and gentle sleep
but still, she misses home.

In Israel, she visits Christ's tomb
and makes new friends,
both Muslims and Jews.
They sip smooth café afuch
or bracing mint, steeped—
and converse about
the many, many things
that they've all seen.

She bids them farewell
and is swept away to Saudi Arabia,
to Medina, to study the Quran—
to find out what Gabriel
told Muhammad—
to imbibe cardamom-infused
Arabic coffee
while contemplating the pages
that led her to these lands.

All over Africa,
her eyes and ears were dazzled
by the many religions and beliefs
which pepper the birthplace of humanity.
Christian and Islam, familiar and fruitful,
and Voodoo and Santeria
had nuggets of golden truth for her.
Rich, red rooibos beckons her to remain,
but home is singing an unusual refrain.

Returning to her birthplace,
she stopped in Salem
to catch her breath,
and learned of both real witches
and the falsely accused
who burned for their beliefs
over the fear of a few.
She celebrated a Sabbat,
dipped an athamé into a chalice of mead,
and consecrated a circle of salt
to the God and to the Goddess.

Returning to her hometown and
the familiar faces she'd always known,
things seemed smaller because she'd grown.
She held bits and pieces of each religion in her breast,
in her heart and her mind, in her hands and her chest—
but what she found in the end
is that her religion is love—
that there may or may not be an afterlife,
that all that matters is what is done.

Kelley Ann Hornyak

TIME WAVES

Sometimes their voices,
just up the stairs,
travel down—
a waterfall of light
through time waves—
transporting me
instantly
to an era
where we
were all happy.

Their frequency
is youthful and juiced,
animated and charged,
and I plug in
to that sparking socket,
unafraid of the potential zap
because, if I'm lucky, it may
set me aflame too.

How long has it been
since I've burned with life?

I am closer to the fire
but it's still beyond the barrier.
A line that I,
in theory,
can never cross.

I am nearer
yet they burn brighter
and I wonder where I lost
the bit that should still glow.

I'll cobble together
a new techno shine,
likely LED,
no warmth,
but so bright.
I'll borrow a smidge
of their leftover magic
and I'll sparkle into the night.

INBORN

There are themes
that sink through things
and anchor me
to times gone by—

to the concept of fate,
of destiny, of divine design—

clear signs
this scientific mind
still can't deny.

Or were they mere branches?
Simple and mappable pathways
that my talents and preferences decide?

Only logical progression
of a body and a mind?

But there are things innate—
ingrained, inborn.
Genetic code or
a creator's brainstorm?

Something tells me
both are true.

I cannot know,
so pondering will do.

SPRING

Stretch

toward the light

toward the sun

toward the energy

that we come from.

Spring

is in the air

is in the mums

is in the wind

and it is warm.

Kelley Ann Hornyak

Sprawl

beneath the clouds

beneath the plums

beneath the gods

and feel the hum.

Sing

to blooming flowers

to crawling worms

to flying birds

and just become.

SOFTEN ME

Light, fragrant, emollient.
Sink within and soften me.

Heal my flesh of battle scars.

Fuse my bones with strength to run.

Fill my hurting heart with joy.

Show me how to live again.

I can create beauty,
but first you must lead me.

I can achieve,
but first I must be.

Teach my words to sing.

Love me as I am.

Accept me when I change.

Allow my soul to fly.

I can love,
but first you must love me.

We can dance,
but first set me free.

PASSIONFLOWER

Passionflower,
I love your bloom.
My eyes rivet,
every spring,
on your blazing
purple shock of life
and on the youth
you bring.

Like a honey kiss
or the quickest lick
off a twist of lime.
So sweet and sharp,
so juicy and thick.
You are bracing bliss.

My soul rises from sleep
and darts like lightning to you,
my sugared slice of paradise.
Igniting me, you reveal your theme.
Erotic and tropical, you want me to be.
I tremble, afraid, but you're so alive
that pieces of me long dead revive.

The scent of a laguna breeze
is blown through ocean curls.
I breathe, renewed,
so filled by you,
so open, so unblue.

I taste your spirit
on islands you've been to,
and wait for you
to bloom again.

Kelley Ann Hornyak

LOVE NOTE

Cutting that cord was like shutting
off my air supply. I never knew
how central you were. How essential.
I thank God for the healing, for the
bridge that connects us. Now I cherish
you like an antique love note printed
with fading ink on disintegrating paper.
I pray for permanence. With you I breathe.

I HAVE A VOICE

I have a voice
and I haven't been using it.

I've been tumbling through
page after page
of personal pain,
and maybe that will help someone,
but there is a larger aim.

I'm a singer,
a lyricist,
a poet,
a writer.
I am female.
Feminist.
LGBT.
Anti-racism.
Anti-bullying.
Cannabis activist.
I am all these things.
So many passions,
so many dreams.

Kelley Ann Hornyak

It is easy to dive headlong
into the tragedies that shaped me
individually,
but writing about
the larger causes that drive me
will challenge,
will strengthen,
will heal
myself and others.

Beyond a tweet,
beyond a blurb,
I should be unafraid
to pen volumes
on the topics
that most need
to be heard.

I have a voice
and I will use it.

SILENT MOVIES

Dandelions.
Daisies.
Sunlight from the east
through morning lark squints
and wide night owl eyes.
Laughter.
Pretty presence—
mindlessness and mindfulness—
the kind that only a child
can access
and innocently
take for granted.
Smiles.
Signs.
Love and lies.
Secrets gold and wise.
The village mockingbird
and the Cape May warbler—
both still babies, both still sweet.
Cartoons and popsicles,
coloring and singing.
Holidays and lucky stars,
rush-rushing, spellbound,
toward the promise of a new day.
Silent movies now,
but vibrant and booming back then.
I'll bring the yellow fingerpaint
and you bring the banana daiquiris.
The dandelions and daisies
are right where they used to be.

Kelley Ann Hornyak

WALLS DON'T TALK (BUT WE SHOULD)

Shimmers and sparkles
on handmade waves—
our own private aqua lake
with tiles that glimmer
in the glaring sun
and underwater walls
that don't talk
even if we're too young
to think the thoughts
and walk the walk.

Purple sky above crackling,
promising more than princely rain.
Storms rolled in—
we'd defy,
we'd swim.
Mermaids never go in.
We never, ever did.

Glowing ectoplasmic lights
cut through the water
and through the night.
Overhearing adult conversations
and knowing that we'd hopefully seen more
than even they would ever see—
that we were damaged
but ecstatically free
in a different way
than they could
ever be.

Emerald in that oceanic blue,
your abandoned opal misses you.
Let's talk amongst the tiles
and watch the stars cross the sky.
Let's let go and not ask why.

4 U

In memory of Prince Rogers Nelson (1958–2016)

What does it mean
when UR energy's
still living in me?
When the echoes
of electricity
still flash
like lightning?

But I am asleep.
Dead to my surroundings.
I'm faltering and floundering
in fitful, painful dreams,
and I don't know what
the point could B.

Not if
I die
here
2.

Not if I die
2 soon
like
U.

Wasn't there a reason?
Wasn't there a time?
I could have sworn
I wanted it enough
to build it with my mind.

But now
UR gone
and I'm
clean out
of time.

If letting go
was the lesson,
why instill
so much passion?

But if God is love,
then take me with U.
I'll love the best
and worst sides of U.
I'll never again
B blind 2 the truth.
And if we live again,
I'm coming back down
4 U.

Kelley Ann Hornyak

EVERY BLESSED THING

I hold all your memories
like a locket long forgotten.
I'm resting in the musty, dusty
box of antique jewels
until crying eyes
fix on a hint of glint
and hurting hands
discover what's within.

I keep all your secrets too,
like a journal burnt to ashes.
I blow in the gusty, blustery
season's swirl of storms
until descendants
breathe in a bit of soot
but successors
cannot cut to the root.

I bear all the weight for you,
last century's good wife times two.
I smother under the bed covers
with other lovers
until I join you
six feet deep in sleep
where I'll let go
of every blessed thing.

THE MOURNER AND THE CORONER

The line between life and death
feels so much thinner
surrounding each loss.

One careless step and I could be
dancing with you on the other side—
toe tags and body bags on this side.

But the sad part
is that at these times,
I really wouldn't mind.

Regrets, yes,
but fearless.

The gate is just a gate—
the goodbye just a goodbye.

And I hate myself when I feel that way,
but somehow I also feel more alive.

I'm more aware of each breath I take—
of the heart that beats and the one that breaks.
I'm the mourner at the viewing—
the coroner downtown undoing
all the tangled truths
that hold the proofs
that just don't matter now.

Kelley Ann Hornyak

A day will come
when I won't be numb,
but another will follow—
one final tomorrow.

Tell me again
how to live
before I die.

COCOON

In memory of Christina Grimmie (1994–2016)

Did your sky come crashing down on you tonight?
Did the heavens open up just to rain blood into your eyes?
Did you cry but find your vision's yet to clear?
I wish that something I could say
could take away your fear.

I have slept inside the chalk lines
and felt tired fingers let go of time.
But I bring no comfort
because I still don't know why.

Cool and breathless is the night
that steals one heartbeat
to break so many lives.

I'll lie in my bed tonight, mindless yet triggered.
What a strange and thoughtless choice of words.
You'll play and rewind—pay every time—
and never forget what you saw and heard.

There are no answers.
May death be a cocoon—
a rite of passage to rebirth.

Kelley Ann Hornyak

TAKE LIFE

Time waits for no one
and it will not wait for me.
Even if I pridelessly beg and plead,
the globe spins beneath my knees
and we keep hurtling through the universe—
forward, onward, linear—
circles, spirals, cyclical—
however you view it,
it's still going to do it.

Stuck in the past, running on fumes—
living in the future, castles or ruins.
All that matters and all that exists
is what we can grab with these fists.
Right now, in the present,
is where you'll find your gifts.

Even when the day brings pain,
it's what we're here for.
We weren't promised pleasure
nor guaranteed glittery treasure.
I'm ready to take life on an as-is basis.
I'm ready to accept the experience,
whether it's lengthy and difficult,
cut short but without tumult,
or some remixed mashup of the two.

I'm stronger now
and wiser somehow.
I'll do what I have to do.

MASK

The mask is ornate—
giant diamonds inlaid,
24-karat gold as a frame,
and the eyes that fall upon it
are green—an emerald so supreme,
if you know what I mean.

It is awe-inspiring.
It is one of a kind.
And it is heavy.
Deceptively heavy.

Still, I cherish this facial armor
that presents itself as an accessory.
I've worn it for a lifetime
and don't know what features
may lie beneath it.

Perhaps none.
Perhaps I am no one
and nobody is home.

No.
I tell lies.
I have seen myself bare as bone,
scraped to nakedness,
and I am as gem-studded spiritually
as this weight-of-the-world covering.

Kelley Ann Hornyak

I could rise to the heights either way—
stripped of adornments or swimming in gold lamé.
I could alternate between the two
depending on my swinging moods,
and still fly to the moon.
But I stay here in this room.

I've got some plans to jot and boxes to tick
before I set my heart aflame
and make my life more than a list.
I'll begin by loving both the costume and my skin—
by sharing the performance
and the one who resides within.
I will not let past chapters dictate what's on this page.
I'll walk heavy when it's worth it
and I'll disrobe to escape.

UNAUTHORIZED

I have a reputation for living life easy and free.
It's rarely been that way—not in reality.
They wonder where I got my talent
but I was groomed by novelists
crafting a biography
so unauthorized.

If I leave no child, no blood legacy,
will it matter how the rest remember me?
Is truth not the goddess that I believed she was?
Is there any record of these lives?

After all—after all—after all,
I am breathing—I am safe.
What comes next just might rebuild
the bridges that had to break.

Had to burn.
Had to learn.

They would never understand if I taught a 101.
I could implant chips but even then it can't be done.
You could erect towers to the dreams that died for them.
Not even then—not even then.

I'll seek the solace they believe I've always held.
I'll whittle the life they fantasize has already been mine.
I'll be bold and bizarre, summer cruel and winter far,
and I'll outdo their fiction from the page to the stage.

Kelley Ann Hornyak

So tabloid trash me.
Go on, bash me.
I am not afraid.
There's nothing you can say
that the waves won't wash away.

TURNTABLES ('ROUND THIS WAY)

Inspired by Judy Rodman

The northeast expanse seems an impassable cold space—
to you, a southwest summer's drive to the good old days.
The landscapes we paint with our words or lack thereof
could be collaborations of celebratory shouts or silence.
The actions we take from each side spell the difference
between a tragic ending and a triumph we've never seen.

The concept that we are separate has been disproven.
For a time, we viewed each other from disparate peaks.
We slept in the valley on certain autumn afternoons,
but only when it softly rained or beneath a certain moon.
We predicated our passion on it proving to be evanescent
but believe me when I say this open door is only yours.

The battle wore us all, now didn't it? Though you started it
with intent to build yourself up and break my dreams down.
I didn't believe the lighthouse keeper when she said to me
it was jealousy—gleaming green jealousy—emerald envy.
Here I stand in the tower, inhaling the breathtaking scene,
and I see that she was right. So were you. And I was too.

Well meaning, you warned me not to give my heart to fools.
I clipped along at a lightning-like pace. I cried continuously.
I kept a bleeding organ on a tear-stained crimson sleeve
and wondered why you were so much more joyful than me.
I had to come 'round your way, steer my steed to your street,
to see embracing reality is not so tragic, just bittersweet.

Kelley Ann Hornyak

Your records spin on segregated turntables. You don't play
well together and often you just don't bother to play at all.
All these circles—all these grooves—all these cycles—
still dictated you can't print your lyrics on the same page.
But I'll forever be the needle, decoding wax messages
and interpreting the vestiges of so many good intentions
while speakers sing of lovely things we never manifested.

MAIMED

I hesitate to put pen to paper on this.
The page repels my hand.
The issue contorts my mind.
I am at a loss in so many ways.
I wonder if it's even worth exploring.
A monologue is the problem
and a conversation is the answer.
Maybe. If there is a solution at all.

I was born and raised in an ignorant land,
shaped and molded by hateful hands,
but I flourished into something loving anyway.
Coated in an impenetrable wax of faith and kindness,
the rains of judgment beaded and never touched me.
I withstood the dark times and still sought the sun.
I must remember this now—must repeat it and repeat it
until muscle memory kicks in and I recreate it.
Recall the motivations and reenact the movements
until it's possible to perform an encore of that victory dance.

Kelley Ann Hornyak

But even the words I choose offend my senses.
Victory? That reeks of battles and of war.
Can you defeat the beast if you become the monster?
I'm not sure of that, or of anything, anymore.
Abhorring the game doesn't mean it won't be played.
Protesting the system won't stop it—not today.
There is reality to be faced
and our euphoric view won't change
the villains who now own the landscape.
Tell me how the peace lovers and the warmongers
can exist in the same physical space.
Tell me how to fix what has been maimed.

2017

PEARLS

If I had been told that I'd spend
my whole life missing you,
I'd still have chosen to fall that hard
and for you to crush my beating heart
because poetry doesn't write itself
and compelling chapters
aren't born of happy times.

Your energy still powers the prologues
and pumps through the pages,
and though there's nothing new to tell,
no other muse feeds me so well.
I have no regrets, regardless of what you think.
I will never apologize for conceptualizing
so many soft pearlescent portraits
of this hard, unforgiving thing.
An eye for beauty is an asset
in times of ugliness and uncertainty.
You made me better.
You made me me.

Kelley Ann Hornyak

Where I used to lament the pain
and wonder how life could be so cruel,
I now thank a higher power
for knowing better than I do.
The more wrinkles that crease my face
and that decorate the spines of my books,
the more thankful I become
for the hurt that brought me—
dancing, flailing—
to my knees
and eventually
to these dreams.

WEIGHTED

A bouquet of feelings:
A quiet understanding.
A wish that I wasn't there.
An annoyance at redundancy.
An awareness that I'm dead.

As empty and unattached as a mind can be,
I swirl down the drain and don't give a damn.
I used to care so much—too much.
Now I couldn't possibly care enough.

The wearing really does wear you down.
You can't swim in the green and not be jaded.
You can't love the beast without wanting to tame it.
You can't wear the crown without being weighted.

I didn't leave a legacy
because our legacy is crazy.
I won't fake a masterpiece
when words are free.

Kelley Ann Hornyak

CHAMPION

God and love—
and love of God—
were so important to you
that even those who weren't religious
became believers of the gospel
when it was read by you.
Out of our graduating class,
you were the one we all believed
would keep his head on straight
and stay clean.

Most likely to succeed
and to do it his own damn way.
Plaques and trophies
emblazoned with
your name and a yesteryear
fill the glass cases in the hallway
not because you're gone
but because you were here.

The field is still on fire,
the bleachers never empty—
or at least that is the way it looks to me.
The victory song still plays all night long
and I'm still the girl with the dream.
We've still got the championship team.

But after the bell grinds out its last note
and I walk the familiar path home by rote,
the Polaroids fade and the tape unwinds.
I perceive the difference between reality and my mind.
Though you're our hometown legend
and you live beyond the bounds of your own life,
the glory is glitter pretending it's gold.
We can be philosophized but not consoled,
and in the end, you were right about the cold.

Kelley Ann Hornyak

MELANCHOLY

Age brings a softness—a shadowy shade
midway between darkness and light.
It paints the undersides of billowing clouds,
underscores laugh lines of tired eyes,
and chases away bleached-blonde highlights.

Swooping in and stealing time—
vultures with fluffy dove feathers.
They comfort even as they subtract life.

The melancholy becomes suitable and familiar—
a worn pair of jeans with the knees long gone.
We don't reach for the rush of fresh, unspoiled love.
We don't mourn our innocence or our trust.

But most of all, we forgive.
We cast doubt to the wind—
we live and let live.

And when our time comes,
they'll be able to say
that we left on good terms.
That we repaired all that shattered.

THE SQUARE CIRCLE

Let me walk with you this evening
along this quiet block

where everything that means anything
is contained in a glowing box—

where blonde sisters trick their misters,
enduring through an immortal age
and bellowing laughter through smoky sage—

where friends meet at the fountain
and aunts visit with their grandbabes—

where the skyline hints at a downtown dream
of honest ad execs and ethical news teams—

where the beach inspires silver ladies
to tell all our truths and coax us out of youth—

where the problems are solved
before you can blink your eyes.

Let me talk with you tonight
and escape my tired mind.

Let me walk with you
and leave this world behind.

DISRUPT THE NIGHT

Summer storm,
replete with rain,
with hail that threatens
to crack the panes.

Flashes light up the navy sky
and the ground takes the hit
like the champ that it is.

You sleep peacefully by my side
while I watch nature disrupt the night.

The warning will pass.
This all will pass.
All that truly lasts
is love.

COMPLIANCE

Was it random fortune or set-in-stone fate
that led me to this broken yet bountiful place?
I eulogized childhood dreams on this gravel
and watched as hope seeped
into the ground like spilled blood.
Still, the meaning of my days and nights
is wrapped around the branches and trunks
and it lifts me up into the moonlight
where my mind shines
even as my body dies.

I adore this lonely dwelling
even though it killed me twice.

I could run or I could declare war.
I could hide. I could wear a disguise.
Instead I assimilate.
I don the gear and cock the weapons.
I learn the lingo and I shoot the shit.
I think I'm getting the hang of it.

I hate to say that they were right,
but glossing and primping a dead body
will never make it come to life.
There's comfort in the coldness—
a certain honesty in the lies.
We may be decomposing,
but I'm damn sure it's our time.

Kelley Ann Hornyak

GOOD ENOUGH TODAY

Once, it seemed smart.
Once, it seemed safe.
Later, it still seemed fun enough
to warrant the risk, to warrant the pain.
But now I pay and I pay and I pay.
I long for a moment that doesn't feel this way.
I thirst for a summer that feels like it should,
where the company is family
and the food is really good—
not just good to my taste buds
but good for my soul,
home cooked and happy,
made with love,
freshly grown.
I don't want to time travel.
I want to fix the here and now.
Regrets have no place at this table
but there's always room for hope.
We've all made multiple mistakes
but we know forgiveness is a breath away,
and even though nothing will ever be the same,
it's good enough—it's good enough—
goddamn, it's good enough today.

AMETHYST

Amethyst era—
another cloak of mourning,
but this one royal and regal.
Translucent and revealing—
this shroud is not just devastating,
but devastatingly sexy.

I am not the cowering child
that I was last time I loved then lost you.
I will not weaken myself to survive you
and I know I am not weaker without you.

Ultraclear armor that glistens and amplifies
the sunlight that passes through it.
Rock solid yet glasslike,
it is both amp and mic—
cavernous crystal canyons
that naturally echo
whatever I bellow.
Reality is as pageworthy
as any fiction I could have crafted,
and from here, I'll only sing songs of truth.

Crescent moon, recharge me, rebirth me.
Re-envision the original dream.
Bring to life all brand new things.
Wrap me up in silken wings.
I'll neglect to nostalgically reminisce
and regret nothing except disallowing bliss.

Kelley Ann Hornyak

I will emerge from this twilight-tinged cocoon
even more beautiful than on the day I was born,
naked of the layers I once encased myself in,
liberated from the loyalty I once lived within.

Amethyst era—
violets over violence.
Chrysalis over crisis.
I'll do more than survive this.

SKY-BOUND

Something I've loudly struggled with
is that my life comes down to this.
The dreams I built up in the air
were left without any doors,
and worse, with no stairs.

I abandoned myself in the way
that so many others taught me to.

Like the child separated from their parent
in the winding aisles of the department store,
I'm left to look and wonder why I'm so forgettable.
I'll hold that thought till evidence convinces otherwise.
I'll take the job and stock the shelves while I muffle cries.

But in the back of my mind, behind broken hearts and lies,
I birth the fresh knowledge that this is a desirable life.
It is not the castle that I constructed cloud by cloud,
but it is a daydream or workday fantasy
that once was out of reach for me.

I might just wrap my arms around
something normal, simple, safe.

And on the way, as I go,
I may find a mountain path
that reaches to an open window
into the star-clad sky-bound paradise
I long ago conceptualized in a faraway life.

Kelley Ann Hornyak

OLD HAUNTS

I left you here because I know you'll be happy
in the orange forest glen beneath the tree canopy.
I left this note in your pocket to explain it all away—
the reasons I could never fill the shoes you carry.

I watched you trip the light fantastic amid dandelions.
I waited as you approached in your mystic hallowed time.
I played the fool just to hear your laughter bubble to the sky.
But time has changed me. I'm worn and weary.

You wrote me rambling love letters that lifted me,
poetry sprawling sexily and unselfconsciously on the page.
You could see us in our old haunts and finding new alcoves.
I could see old habits and they die just as quick as love.

I wonder if, in time, you might forgive me—
forget transgressions of an old yet ageless man.
When you wake and find this hand-scrawled letter,
search your heart for strength to understand.

NEON BEACH

Bass licked by tropical tones—
sunset tinged with candy ribbons.
Melodies fill up my sea and my sky
and I run over with temptations.
Once, this space was empty.
Twice, this space was home.

I thought I'd tasted the last bit of thrill
and I was content to leave before the encore.
All too willing to drift into the star-packed night,
dozing through the drive, unconscious of the road home.
The last thing I longed for
was to stay and sip and sway—
to groove into the midnight hour,
finding neon patterns between the notes
and tracing God's blueprints with sandy toes.

I thought I was too worn and frayed
to last till the morning—to share this sunrise.
To let conversation tumble and laughter bubble.
To watch powder blue waves lap at the shore
while loving the moment and planning for more.

Kelley Ann Hornyak

But the muse has been good to me
and she returned with full bottles
and plenty of hot coals.
She won't pour the drinks
and she won't stoke the fire,
but she'll provide and wait patiently
for me to smile at the responsibility.
It isn't effort when it's done lovingly.
It isn't work when you love the dream.

I'll sleep on the beach
with your arms encircling me.
I'll wake when the band begins to play.

BRAVE

The chaos rips through the air,
sending sheets of ocean
wildly against our comfort zone.
The tropical storm returns home.

Placid moments hint at violence
but between the sheets,
we still sing of love.
There will be no end of us.

While the eye is centered, deadly,
let me crack a window
and let's climb outside just for a time
to feel the void and comprehend
that one day we will live again.

While our dreams are sleeping soundly
and the bravest of the brave still share our space,
we will pause and breathe and play,
building hope from these dark days.

When we let go, we'll let go,
and we'll love whatever lands we turn up in.
We'll burn your candle brightly
and ink your patterns forever on our skin
so you will recognize us when we meet again.

Kelley Ann Hornyak

THE THINGS I'VE SEEN

Dedicated to the victims and survivors of mass shootings

The moon is close to fullness as she dances among the clouds
and the night is as lovely as it always is and always was.
We hold hands and converse as if nothing has changed,
but we know that beneath the sidewalk runs a river of blood —
the satellite maps littered with slices and bullet holes.

Beneath the beauty, there has always been death,
but where it used to just be a timely passing,
it is now cruelty that underlies everything.
An ever-present, dinging, flashing hint
that we might not make it home tonight.

Somehow, we keep breathing.
Those left pick themselves up and keep living.
But you're lying if you say you're unchanged.
I'd be lying if I said I ever felt safe.

Do we accept that we're living in a war zone?
There are changes that can be made
but we can't bring bodies back to life
and we can't ever make things right.

The media creates a paranoia
that feeds already sick minds.
No one is immune to it.
I don't know how to integrate
what I see on the screen
with my daily reality.
I don't know how to heal
from the things I've seen.

Kelley Ann Hornyak

VISIBLE

You are long gone.
I don't recall your face,
but I remember your flowers.
Across the street, the acorns still fall
and no one sweeps them away,
just like back in the day.
But your house is different
and I wonder if you can see it.
The new family that moved in
tore out the driveway
and turned your garage
into a living room.
A new driveway and garage
are behind it—a new patio too.
I'm not one to embrace change,
but it's lovely, what they've done.
The trees are still as majestic
and the space feels alive,
like it kept your energy.
Maybe the tulips still exist,
tangible to my soul
but not to my eyes,
blowing invisibly
when the wind
sails on by.
Perhaps
nothing
really
ever
dies.

OPPOSING SIDES

The classic tales will lead a child to believe
that reality and wishes are on opposing teams,
that desires and dreams differ
from day jobs and responsibilities,
and that yesterday and today
cannot be printed on the same page.

In the stillness of a better dimension,
I find that these concepts are allies
and in fact do not fight on opposing sides.

What inner revolution might occur
if I accepted both my cravings
and the nourishment I receive —
if I embraced both the ultimate
and the most mundane in me?

So I stop resisting.
I integrate my two halves
and my myriad facets.
Let them gleam,
let them shine
in the light.

I am loving.
I am loved.
I am enough.

Kelley Ann Hornyak

BREAK

I had to write it out of me till I could let it go.
This broken heart will beat for you no more.
Where once I saw strings of twinkle lights,
magical moonbeams, and mistletoe,
I now see only a desolate land of snow.

Let me die in the ice fields
because I was too pure for you.
You were right to believe you were bad for me,
just not for the reasons you'd think.
Your red-eye flights were the poison,
not the snowflakes you dance in.
Your departures were my breaking points.
The cracks became canyons—
the wind, tornadoes.

Now and then, under a cobalt moon,
enough is enough for me too.
It is part of aging—this changing.
This newfound respect for my being.
It will be strange to cut the ties this time,
knowing that the heartstrings are only mine.

BICOASTAL

In loving memory of Geraldine Adeline Prieur (1941–2019)

Your noble bay is empty of its curative waters
but these islands are awash with emotion—
a sensitive sympathy, a motherless melancholy.
I'll keep it quiet, keep it modest, keep it to myself
because if I never said I loved you,
it makes no sense to say I'll miss you.

But every breath you took mattered
and I'm marinated in memories
that you've long since forgotten.
It's too late to change the time
so some acceptance is in order,
but I do regret a thing or two
and I admit the fault was mine.

I was the textbook only child,
unsure of how to interact
and lost in her own mind.
I was angry that you loved the others
differently than you loved me.

If only I'd given you a window to observe my madness—
to get a grip on the energy that makes me tick.
It wouldn't have changed things between us that much
but it would have meant that I was present—that I tried.
And any animosity between us would have been
based on what is real instead of on rumors and lies.

Kelley Ann Hornyak

Regardless, where we are feels right.
There's a lightness in the love now,
something I sought but could not create.
It is natural and built by time itself.
From where I sit, I must let go
and accept what we are
as well as what we were.

We're so similar in our bicoastal estates—
too similar in so many ways.
Too focused on what we can't change.
Too separate, both soon swept away.

LET ME BE

Here it is.
The letting go.
The chapter closing.
The clench unfolding.

What broke within
remains in pieces,
but also at peace,
the way it should be.

I rest.
I breathe.
I dream.

Future pages may bring the closure I seek
or they may just bring more tragedy to me.
Maybe even something frustratingly in-between.
But I won't try to manipulate the possibilities.

Here, I am not the writer.
I accept what fate has deemed
fitting for my story arc
and poetic for the screen.

I let you go
to let me be.

Kelley Ann Hornyak

THE LAND OF LOVING ME

No matter what,
from here on out,
I'm taking care of myself.

Seasons and seasons of putting others first
and focusing on outside perceptions
instead of what I think and feel
has led me here,
to the land of loving me
and moving confidently along.

I can invest my time and energy
and still not have you see me.
I can explain until I'm blue
but you'll still view me through
a lens of you.

That used to make me see red —
make me charge through our dynamic
like a Taurean rushed to change.
But let me settle into my Scorpion ambition
and hone in on the grand scheme.
It's a mystery still
but not a single piece
is what you think of me.

This globe is cold enough
for me to finally understand
that looking out for me
has to come before
caring for you.

You will survive and even thrive,
bettered by the tough love treatment.
I will finally feel this life is mine.

Kelley Ann Hornyak

PEACE & EASE

I'd been told to ignore the sting—
that the point was in the pain.
But my advisors never faced
my particular affliction
and they never lent a hand
nor coated me in any balm.
They meant well
but their counsel
was my downfall.

I began with one small gesture
to alleviate a chronic soul-deep burn—
reached out to another being
with no vested interest
who knew what to say
and what to do.
Overnight, relief was given.
Over time, complete remission.

With one laceration healed,
I was inspired to treat another,
and on and on
till all maladies were gone.

Irritation creates pearls
and pressure creates diamonds.
But I am not a jewel,
I'm a living, breathing person.
I deserve a moment of enjoyment
here on the physical plane.
Keep your worship of hardships
and litanies of adversity.
I'm moving on
to a place
of peace
and ease.

Kelley Ann Hornyak

HATCHET

I never bring you up in conversation
because too many know the truth
and then there are those that still don't.

Those that know would nod and smile
while marveling at how damaged I must be
to forgive the deranged villain of innocence
and choose to cherish past happiness instead.
They would replay memories that belong to me—
videotapes of pain that no one else should see.

Those that I'm sworn to leave in the dark
would praise you without apologetic remark
while I awkwardly hush the parts of my brain
that haven't forgiven and cannot forget.

Those two crowds are enough.
Never mind mixed company.

Your crime does not go unpunished—
I pay and I pay for all that you skipped out on.
The shame somehow rests within me
but only because you refused to wear it.
You could have tried to make amends
but instead it was me who extended pardon
as you left this plane for the kind of place
where all is absolved and maybe erased.

But don't forget there's a hatchet to be buried,
and the only place you'll find dirt is on Earth.
We landscape six feet in place of serenity.
We tend to the trauma while you fly free.

Kelley Ann Hornyak

DISCARDING DARKNESS

Letting go of darkness.
What it's like to try to kiss the hand
that is and always has been intangible.
How it feels to wrap my arms
around a spectre.
Empty.

This day tried to come
a couple of times before,
a decade ago or more.
I wouldn't wake
so it went away.
I thought it might just stay.

Denial was warm and cozy.
Why grieve when I could dream?
But even limitless revisions won't rewrite
a thoughtless thief into a thriller knight.
I can't recover what's been taken
but I can choose not to dwell on the loss.

Before I jump,
I'll process the hell out of this pain.
I'll filter your cruel, noxious poison
till it's sparking water fit to bathe in,
and then I'll let it rain
until every tear is washed away.

Discarding darkness.
Empty.
Room to accommodate
the sun's rays.

Kelley Ann Hornyak

BURN BRIGHT

Depression, is it?
Medication-induced
and difficult to elude?
I assumed the obvious
to be the truth,
but this trouble
is not what it
masquerades
to be.

There is another name
for the emptiness
that steals sleep,
makes allies
into enemies,
and drains
dreams.

Burnout.

I am burnt out—
an empty shell
that was once a home,
consumed by arson,
charred to black—
spirit sent to the sky
in clouds that choke
and mock the moonlight.

But I'm not built from
kindling and logs.
I'm a brick house,
mighty and holding nothing back,
and I do still hold the winning hand.
This was a newsflash and only that.
I can be rebuilt to truly last.

Not a terminal disease—
a temporary disaster.
A gift disguised as destruction
and an order with no instructions.

But angels sleep upon the ash tonight
and in the morning all will be right.
Dreams will be solid—burnt will be bright.

Kelley Ann Hornyak

BUT I BREATHE

Triggers flashing
like emergency lights—
frightening fireworks,
lightning overworked—
everything burnt on sight.

But I breathe.
Inhale slowly and evenly—
exhale slowly and evenly.

I breathe,
I breathe,
I breathe.

I'm not there.
I'm right here.

No shots were fired today.
No threats were made today.
No health scares today.
Nobody to save.

I breathe,
I breathe,
I breathe.

I take in the current scenery.
I acknowledge who is here with me.
I drop the past
and let it be.
I free the future,
whether banshees or glee.

It's too late to change the time—
too etched in stone to rewrite lines.
And in this moment, that's just fine.
I've seen much worse and kept my spine.

The mines lie in wait to slay,
but they are illusions
and even delusions.
I'll accept what comes today.
I'll breathe, I'll breathe some more,
and come hell or high water—
or heaven and a sunny day—
I'll stay.

Kelley Ann Hornyak

LET IT SHRIEK

Every time I think I'm free
it all comes rushing back at me.
But now I'm worn, my edges blurred.
Might not remember what I heard.
(And if I do, am I really sure?)

The pieces never fit back
the way they did before you broke her.
Before you broke me.
(Was that me?)
It's been so long.
She, me, whoever that child was
is a ghost, a memory.

The blood stains never fade.
Not even with sun—not even with age.
The images remain frozen
(thankfully frozen)
and the pain resides
in the shower
or in sleep.

Obscured by the curtain of water
or beneath the veil of dreams,
I (she?) can cry, even weep,
let it shriek,
let it speak,
let it seep.

The evil that invaded safe.
The night that took her mind away.
The words that remained locked up tight,
taunting her with sleeping memories
and shaping her waking life.

I (she?) can let it go
when no one's looking.
I (she?) can stoke the coals
or let them be.

The lovely girl
still playing with fire.
The lonely girl
still counting her goodbyes.
Which storied headline
will you apply
to my very real demise?

Kelley Ann Hornyak

SANTA BARBARA

This shark-filled sea is as dangerous
as the lightning-lit sky above it,
and the ones I love most
are in harm's way.

The sharks smell blood
and the lightning seeks release,
and I can't reach the little ones
in my sinking dinghy —
can't send out a lifeline
from this distance.

How rough and choppy
these waters turned out to be.
There's nothing pacific
about the waves
of Santa Barbara.

Will rhinoceros skin grow
on these baby mermaids?
It seems that legs may be
more useful in these times.
So much has changed
yet so much is the same.

Poet Iconic, Vol. 1

I pray
and I scream
and I make deals
with devils and gods,
but I feel unheard
and I fear the worst.

I'd give my life
to save these souls.
All I can do is hope
and grow old.

Kelley Ann Hornyak

MILK (TREAD CAREFULLY)

Doesn't it seem deliberately ignorant
that I'm swallowing pills to numb the pain
that my loved ones have thrust upon me,
after having watched you do the same,
after having watched you kill the pain,
watching your family circle the drain,
when all you wanted was to be that clan
and be that strong and hold those hands?

Human relationships are inexplicable.
I'm as lost in them now as I ever was.
I can sense the judgment even in the love.
I don't think anyone will ever understand me
the way that I understood you, unconditionally.
But the magic between us was the super distance,
the miles and miles of mountains and desert
that kept the love from becoming resentment,
that kept the dream enclosed safely in glass
like your awards and baubles and gems.
It kept us sweet. It kept us friends.
With no beginning, we cannot end.
The real can't hold a candle to pretend.

Poet Iconic, Vol. 1

Still I spend day and night studying your moves,
learning new lessons as I watch the same sessions.
Some are honed in school but I was honed by you.
I spin to thrill, swallow a pill, sip that milk, get that ill.
Sleep comes and saves me from the endless mundane,
bringing waves of you to motivate and cleanse away
all the bits of death that cling and suffocate.
I'm not ready to go. I'm just building my stage.
I'm not coming with you. Not yet, anyway.

The fact that encourages and inspires me now
is that the electricity in the air feels like it did then.
When I was born, things were different,
and they're swinging back there again.
Cynical nothing revolves to reveal hopeful everything.
The meaningless is suddenly pumped full of meaning.
And best of all, life is fun. We can play and we can sing.
It's not all about the quota or how much they owe you.
I might just carve that dream into my life's tree,
might just craft that career that sets me free,
might just cull that guiding group that loves me.

Yes, sweetie, for now I will pop that pill and let it soothe me.
But just the type and the amount that the good doc prescribes.
No pill pushers on my roster, no doctor-shopping on my agenda.
And as much as I'd love a yes-man or two
to undo the damage of the endless no-no-no,
I will keep my smart, levelheaded friends at my side
and let no others in our small and well-chosen circle.
You will dance along the outskirts, unbeknownst to all but me.
You will forever fuel my creativity. I'll forever tread carefully.
I'll remain as long as I can, embellishing and gilding our legacy.

HOVEL

Erosion doesn't require abuse.
It only requires neglect.
Lack of money, time, or love—
it doesn't matter which,
and many times, it's all.
In any case,
what was raised in hope
will slowly and tragically fall.
The shingles stay past their intended time—
a few fall off and the rain sinks in.
The ceiling begins to sweat—
the clammy inner skull of the home
perspiring at the nearby knowledge
that soon what it shields
will disintegrate.
The gutters fill with leaves,
then rain, then snow, then ice.
Spring brings green trees and beauty
but also thaws the frozen seasons
that frame the roofline like memories.
Drip, drip, drip, drip,
while you work,
while you sleep,
while you laugh at what's on TV.
The walls sweat like the ceiling before it—
shivering at the understanding
that the paint will soon peel and crack
and the wood will mildew and creak.
The doors swell and warp
as the temperatures rise and fall,

and soon you can't lock up the house
or keep that once-magical portal
on its now rusty hinges.
Windows pop and threaten to shatter—
no one visits or knows what's the matter.
The floorboards stop gossiping
and begin to scream—
the wires fry and pipes burst—
soon you're tip-toeing,
dressing in darkness
and saving coins for the laundromat.
It would cost more to repair
what has been uncared-for
than it would to start fresh
in a clean foreclosure.
But is it a home that we're eulogizing?
Or is it an aging body
or a decades-long relationship
struggling beneath its own valuable weight?
It doesn't matter.
It doesn't matter.
I promise you,
it does not matter.
They're all distressing, all grave—
all natural and to be expected.
Nature taking its course
when we don't put up the good fight
to resist the savage winds of change.
In this era of instant everything on-demand,
we don't know how to continue traditions of the past,
and we've lost the blueprints and instructions
for building and ensuring something lasts.
I pray for one more night
of the roof not falling in
while we bicker and decide

Kelley Ann Hornyak

whether to save this hovel
of a castle we're in.

THE LAUGHING GIRL AND ME

Look again with aging eyes
at a union still youthful, still sweet.
Breathe in. Let it weather. Let it deepen.
Appreciate that we have so much room to grow
and see that as possibility and potential—
see it as promise.

Drift through magical nights in the twinkling glow
between the frost and the year's first snow.
Walk side by side, worn but optimistic.
Savor the slow rekindling
of a love that deserves to live.

Don't regret slaying the demons
that came attached to our broken hearts.
Don't lament the decades of confusion
because that path led to clarity and kindness.
Special indeed is this love thing—
returning to the vibe that saturated our beginning.

We are blessed to be here—right here—
no matter how hard-fought our footing is
or how precarious this position may be.
In this breath, we are together and whole.
In this instant, paired and complete.

Kelley Ann Hornyak

I knew I couldn't live without you,
but I saw it as a unique and beautiful doom.
But no. It is an intricately carved destiny
that heals all things and washes us clean.
A brand new start for the laughing girl and me.

SUMMER TRIPS

I'm sorry I put you in the box, baby.
I'm sorry I labeled you a sexy celebrity
when you were just a hometown flake like me.
You appeal and you break me wide open
and I guess I'm just a glutton
for that kind of button pushing.

I keep gunning the motor with the battery dead.
I keep wishing on stars when the sun's overhead.

Peeling off the burnt-on glasses,
I can see that I'm far from the ingénue
that pens these lamenting love letters to you.
Wrinkles singed into changing skin,
scars slashing the flesh.
I'm less than a catch.

And though we won't see eye to eye,
I'll press forward, sketching pretty lies.
You play the champion to my protagonist.
I like to pack a little fiction for my summer trips.

Kelley Ann Hornyak

SKATE OR DIE

The night after he left us, I skated on the shadow side.
I watched the stars spin like teacups in the sky.
The angels serenaded him through staticky airwaves
and I made wishes on every star in sight.

The pain returned when wishes merely dangled,
so many years gone by and then a chance.
I slept through the silence
and missed out on the sunshine,
but after I heard your voice,
I took a dive.

The stars were in the waves this time,
aqua healing points of light.
They swept over me
and I felt almost all right.

But disembodied voices can't soothe each other's hurts
and wishes don't measure up against work.
The path gets longer but it's never too far.
I would walk it for you if you wanted me to.
Instead I'm writing to you
or to the memory of you.

Tears could wash away the blood stains.
Laughter could take the tears.
Unstuck, we could move on
and keep on till we're gone.

PAPER DREAMS

Can you imagine how much love
is woven through these trees for you?
Through these small town streets
where I drive and sing and dream,
where I fantasize and romanticize
about lovers who never loved me?
It is heartbreakingly beautiful,
even if your eyes can't perceive
all the strings of heart beads
and streamers of paper dreams.
How lucky you were
to be loved so greatly
and yet how tragic
to be light-years away
from this heartbeat.

STAR CHARTS

Body aches—
psychotic breaks.

It's a damn shame
what they did to us.

Did we come down for this?
Did we chart it all
amongst the stars
and choose
this time
and place?

When we slip between the covers
and wake up in another dimension,
will all this chaos blend with heaven
and make the most flawless sense?

Will every scar
lead to someone else's victory?
The butterfly effect
is good enough reason for me
if it's rooted in meaningful destiny.

But I'd come back down
to this hell all over again
to save you from your pain.

May the grand plan
keep us hand-in-hand
through the lifetimes
and may they
be better
and better
and better still.

Kelley Ann Hornyak

PASS FOR HUMAN

Moody as the clouds rolling over this Halloween moon,
I'm not the greatest company tonight.
In a room full of dancing and laughter,
I move in slow motion between the dancers,
unnoticed in my melancholy haze.

The faces are familiar but it all feels so different.
Certain words feel misplaced
and I just don't fit in this space.
I could play the game until the veil thinned—
could get along and pass for human.
Now my fangs are clear to see
if only they would look at me.
Thank goodness they don't look at me.

I slip out the sliding door
and into the arms of the night.
I dart between the fog on the street
and obscure myself behind light posts
as children pass by at their most merry.
These costumed kids should not be told
of what lies ahead when they grow old.
I could function as a warning label
or a crimson road type of instructional video.
The kind that traumatizes more than it helps.
But I'm here to save myself on this particular All Hallows' Eve.
They'll get no wisdom or guidance from the likes of me.
It's best if I keep making ground,
sharp teeth hidden by my frown.

I don't know where the moon will lead me.
I have no map and no one like-minded beside me.
Settling into the darkness is as scary as it is comforting,
like giving birth or being born
and facing the cold and unforgiving unknown.
I stalk serenity but compulsively creep.
I yearn for rest but cannot risk sleep.
I'll don this cloak, perform this smoke and mirrors show
if it means surviving till the stark morning—
learning to live in the light,
teeth bared and claws out.

ABOUT THE AUTHOR

    Kelley Ann Hornyak is a poet and writer from Allen Park, Michigan. Her work centers on themes of love and loss, healing and acceptance. She has been featured in the literary journal *Andwerve* and is a past winner of The Christina Aguilera Poetry & Art Contest from DoSomething.org. Much of her poetic body of work can be read on her blog, *PoetIconic.com*.

www.ingramcontent.com/pod-product-compliance
Lightning Source LLC
Chambersburg PA
CBHW051350070526
44584CB00025B/3708